FROM THE
GROUND UP

FROM THE

GROUND UP

7 PRINCIPLES FOR BUILDING A BUSINESS FAST

SUNIL KUMAR

A catalogue record for this book is available from the National Library of Australia

Disclaimer

CONTENTS

'While most people only dream of a life filled with personal success and professional achievement, few get to actually make it a reality. But Sunil Kumar has taken it one step further. Not only has Sunil built an award-winning business from the ground up with his bare hands, he has also broken down his learnings into a repeatable framework that we can all use to build our own empires. This book outlines the seven principles that have been decoded from Sunil's years of hard work, extreme personal sacrifice and relentless professional growth … and all you have to do is to follow it just one step at a time to achieve your own goals, on your own terms.'

Sharran Srivatsaa, CEO of Srilo Capital

'No matter what business you're in Sunil's book will give you large a number of practical, fast-growth strategies you can implement immediately. Do yourself a favour and invest a few hours reading this book.'

John McGrath, Founder & Executive Director,
McGrath Estate Agents

'A truly inspirational story of a young migrant who built his company into one of the top 10 fastest growing companies in Australia. I am sure this book will inspire millions of young entrepreneurs around the globe.'

Sukhmeet Singh Ahuja, Chief Executive Officer,
ANGAD Australian Institute of Technology

'I coach and train agents in Sunil's business and in this book Sunil covers the essential components of leadership in a modern era'

Tom Panos

'Sunil is one of the most driven and inspired entrepreneurs my team and I at The Entourage have ever worked with. His journey and lessons are an inspiration to any business owner who knows it's not their time to give up, but rather, to take their next big leap in creating a long-lasting legacy.'

Jack Delosa

'I had the pleasure of meeting Sunil and his team when I spoke at their annual conference. He is passionate, driven and leads from the front. He shared the vision and goals with the team, ensuring that he engaged all parts of his business. The enthusiasm, passion and connection of the team was clearly visible on the day.'

Sadhana Smiles (Jeraj),
Director, Harcourts Move

'If you're in business and looking for inspiration and a pathway to grow then you need to read this book! I have personally seen the energy, effort and commitment Sunil has poured into his business journey. *From the Ground Up* distills these amazing life and business lessons together into Sunil's seven principles for growth. An entrepreneur's must read.'

Michael Sheargold,
CEO, RER Network

FOREWORD

When I first met Sunil at a Real Estate Results conference in 2016 I was immediately struck by his sincerity as well as his sponge-like desire to learn as much as he could from not only the conference but everyone there.

While most people were hanging around the bar that first night, I recall sitting in a corner with Sunil having one of the most interesting conversations I have ever had with a fellow Real Estate practitioner. I knew then that this man would go on to do some amazing things.

While reading *From the Ground Up* I was reminded of this first meeting as well as my own journey in establishing and building a business from nothing. It took me back to the ups and downs and the big unknown, but it also made me think of what it takes to be bold enough to truly have a vision and follow it through. Sunil has encapsulated what it takes to turn that vision into a journey of resilience, constant reassessment, and dogged determination to make it happen. There are no excuses here, just a string of constant, 'giving it a go', the subsequent learnings that come from that, and then the practical application of those learnings into action.

Another element of this book that really struck a chord with me was Sunil's desire to enrich the lives of those around him and to empower his team to be the best they can be; in other words, it was not just about him achieving his goals, it became that the goal of the goal was the success of all those within the Reliance family and beyond into the community.

Sunil is unstoppable in his drive to achieve his goals, but he has also learnt along the way to appreciate the greatest gift of all, family, and to stop and smell the roses along the way while always looking after his health and both his physical and spiritual wellbeing.

This book is not only about a journey of discovery, but also a blueprint of how a 'can do' approach has led to the creation of this 'how to' manual for success in business and in life. Not everyone will have the scope of belief and determination that Sunil has, but if you can open your mind to the possibilities of your potential and explore what you can do to have a positive impact on your life then I believe the objectives of why Sunil wrote this book will be achieved.

Enjoy every page, and to get the most out of it make sure you carry out the exercises as you go as learning is all about how much you absorb and then how much you apply.

**John Cunningham, Managing Director,
Cunningham Real Estate, ex president REI NSW**

MY MAIN FOCUS IN BUSINESS IS TO
SERVE. MONEY, POWER, AND PRESTIGE
ARE JUST THE INEVITABLE BYPRODUCTS
THAT HAVE SHOWN UP ALONG THE WAY.

ROBIN SHARMA

INTRODUCTION

February 23, 2013

I woke up, still in my suit. My jacket and trousers were crushed under me and my hair was stuck to my forehead. My head felt heavy. It was almost dark, and as I slowly gained focus, I began to look around. The room was unfamiliar – it wasn't my bedroom; it wasn't even my house. *I felt sick.* Slowly, I began to piece together what had happened a few hours earlier. I was shattered. The ill feeling in my stomach refused to leave. How had things come to this?

It was all to do with an argument with my business partner that turned into a terrible fight. We had opened our very first real estate agency – Reliance Real Estate, Werribee – a couple of years earlier, both investing equal share into the business. Prior to this, we had worked on one project for mutual benefit: looking for any fresh opportunity. This time, we'd found one, identifying a gap in the real estate market in Melbourne's west. I shared my idea with him to open an agency and he offered to join me. It seemed a fantastic move and I was very excited about taking the next step in my career. But instead of learning everything about it first, which is what I usually do, I just jumped in, taking a risk, spurred on by previous success. I felt sure we would not fail.

I resigned from my current role with another agency and leapt into the new venture. I wanted to do right by my former agency, so we went to a completely new area to start from scratch there. We agreed that my business partner would be the equal investor, while I would be 'feet on the ground', doing the work.

Unfortunately, it didn't go well. Two years in, I found myself working for almost no pay, often six and a half days a week. I was exhausted, frustrated and felt like it was all too hard.

I was newly married when I started the business. We had a new house, so there was a mortgage to pay off. I wasn't seeing my family and I wasn't spending enough time with my newborn baby. I knew this business would test me, but I could never have imagined it would test me so deeply.

That day in February 2013, I was feeling stressed, overworked and worried. During the evening that changed everything, my business partner strode into my office. I could see by his face that his mind was made up. He was determined to shut down our business and he blamed me for the failure of the company. He said the venture was making a loss every month, and that there was no point running a company into the ground. He didn't want to invest more of his financial share, because he didn't think he would get it back.

This was totally unfair! Yes, the business we had created together *was* losing money month by month. Yes, there were hardly any clients coming in: no one knew who we were! And as a result, we weren't generating much income. Plus, our key performer had also left.

But I couldn't make him see that businesses take time to grow and that success doesn't happen overnight. Especially in an untapped real estate market in the western suburbs.

I was so passionate about making this work. I tried to raise more money from the bank or other sources. I needed to raise another $30,000 so I could pay some dues and work from the ground up again. But my partner said I was dreaming if I thought I could get the business back up and running.

He demanded we shut it down and stated that if it kept operating, he wouldn't give me any ownership. He was a builder, constructing homes in the western suburbs, and he hardly had time to learn about the day-to-day, ins-and-outs of running a real estate agency. But he believed he knew everything about business. His basic formula was cut costs – pay less to your employees and pretend you were helping your team. He said he would take over from the next month, and that I 'could just go and work for someone else'. He believed that because I was young, it'd be easy for me to just pick up and start somewhere else, suggesting that I could simply uproot my family and go interstate and start again.

We started arguing. How could he be so shortsighted? Success in any new venture takes patience and perseverance.

Surely, he was missing the bigger picture. You can't judge the future based on current events, and I had big plans for Reliance. Oh, I knew that there would be challenges, but I wasn't giving up like he was.

But the arguing was out of hand. At that point, I'd had enough; I reached breaking point. Which is exactly what my business partner wanted.

I am not a person who gets angry easily. But he pressed my buttons by blaming me for everything. He wasn't acknowledging my commitment and perseverance. And when he said I didn't need to come in the next month, that he would take care of things from here, and told me, 'I could just go work for someone else,' I lost it.

I stood up and threw some books off my desk, and then I threw some other things around my office. Every muscle in my body was charged with energy. In that moment, I completely lost my patience, my temper and my conscience all at the same time, which is very uncharacteristic for me.

We had argued before, but never to this extent. He stepped back. This business was everything to me. Giving up was never an option. It was as if someone was trying to take my child away from me. It was just an investment to him, but to me it was my hard work, blood, sweat and tears. He was shocked with my reaction but said he had done what he came to do. And then he just walked out the door, leaving me breathless in the middle of my ruined office.

It was a hot Melbourne evening, 30 degrees at least, and the more I ran over the fight in my head, the hotter the room became, until I thought I was burning from the inside. But soon my anger turned to fatigue. I was exhausted. I put the fan on to try to cool off. My mind was weary, and my body had no energy left to move. I couldn't even step out of the room. The anger had drained me of all my strength and I recognised that this was not a healthy state for me to be in. I couldn't think about going home. I didn't even have the energy to walk.

I lay down on the floor next to my desk, fully dressed in my suit. I felt instantly calmer, *cooler*. Water fell from my eyes thinking about the sheer amount of work I had invested in the business, and these arguments with my partner.

I truly felt like all my dreams were broken, like I didn't have a place in the world anymore. I had made Australia my home – one of dreams and ambition, where I could chase success and a life I could be proud of, for myself and for my young family. Lying on the floor, among the books I'd strewn about, I felt like the world had just ended for me, and I was heartbroken.

I was raising a child (Reliance), putting my heart and soul into it, and someone was going to just come and take it all away from me? But the real tragedy of my 'failure' was that my time and efforts were going to be wasted. I had a baby at home, and because I was spending all of my time on the business, I hadn't seen him much in his first year. Now, all those early mornings and late evenings were for nothing! It was time I could have better spent with my wife and baby, and I felt like it had been stolen from me. I would *never* get that time back.

Was growing a business really meant to be this hard?

I don't remember how and when, but I fell asleep with my thighs tucked childlike into my chest. I slept on the office floor for two hours. When I woke, I was stiff and sore but I gradually unpeeled myself from the carpet. It was dark inside and out. I checked my phone and saw that my wife had phoned me four times. I didn't call her back as I had no answer for her and had no energy to talk.

Years later, when I told her about this, she quietly cried. She said she could see what the company meant to me and how I would have felt at the time. I wasn't proud of my angry reaction, but it has since become the most significant business moment in my life.

★

Fast forward to 2021. That same failing business – Reliance Real Estate – is recognised as ranking and winning Australia's fastest growing real estate group three years in a row in the *Financial Review's* 'Weekly Fast 100 List' as well as in the *Business Review Weekly*.

I was elated! I had never given up on my dream and now it was paying off, but the speed in which we were achieving this was mind-blowing.

In 2018, we won ARERA's (The Australasian Real Estate Results Awards) Agency of the Year award for Australia and New Zealand,

and I was awarded Principal of the Year by ARERA for the third time before being inducted into the Hall of Fame. That was on top of winning ARERA's Rising Star Agency of the Year award in 2018.

Now we have a head office in Point Cook, in Melbourne's west. We have nine branches spread throughout Melbourne's growing western suburbs, and we recently acquired a major agency, one of our biggest competitors, within our core area of business.

We have grown from humble beginnings to 10 offices and a team of nearly 140 strong, all with a shared vision, all enjoying success in our personal and professional lives, and all committed to helping others and in helping over 4500 families to fulfil their property dreams every year.

In 2016, we established the Reliance Foundation, providing a platform for the team to contribute to local charities through salary sacrifice and fundraising efforts.

I have learnt so much over the last ten years. I am a proud Indian immigrant, who arrived in a new land, with no experience in the industry, and I have developed into an award-winning profes-sional at the helm of one of the fastest growing businesses in Australia. I am a loyal husband and now a delighted father of two beautiful children.

I was able to stay strong in my belief that this business was worth fighting for, and that I could take it all the way in a few short years. But business can be tough. And let's face it, succeeding in any industry is hard work and requires a lot of effort. Just look at the statistics. The percentages vary from country to country and industry to industry, but as per the Australian Bureau of Statistics, more than 60% of small businesses stop their operation within the first three years of their start-up journey.

When things are working beautifully in your company, it's a different story. When you are making profit, your team is performing and people are starting to notice your achievements, the outlook is sunny and anything seems possible. You enjoy the life you want to live and enable others to do so, too.

There's nothing more rewarding than feeling you're building something worthwhile and something that's enabling people to fulfil their dreams. You are making a positive impact on many lives – not just your own.

For me, this is what life is all about. When I stopped and thought about my journey so far, I realised there were many lessons I learnt as a business owner. Yes, you have the freedom to make choices and they are choices that make you feel alive, invigorated, and excited – and ultimately rewarding. But you also must face dark times, too. It can be a lonely journey and you might need to be prepared to stand alone when no one else believes in you. It can be a scary time and you might not be sure whether the thing that you are so passionate about is worth it.

When the odds are against you, how can you make your story a success? What and who can you rely on? How can you build a business that lasts? Where do you start?

In the following pages, I will share with you my seven key principles. They are the simplified principles that have helped my business thrive and contributed to its success. They are the learnings I have applied that have helped Reliance grow into the business it is today.

I share these principles with you in the hope you will benefit and apply them to your own ventures. They are perfect for entrepreneurial business owners who want to build their company from the ground up, from day one, as well as established enterprises to ensure the business flourishes long into the future. The principles will help you achieve your dreams, as well as the dreams of your team and allow you to create a positive contribution to your lives together.

As we take the journey together through each principle, I'll illustrate them with examples of my own experience to show you how you can avoid mistakes and pitfalls and overcome challenges just like I did.

By the end of this book, you will have practical tactics and a deeper understanding on how to run your company more smoothly, enjoy a great connection with your team and develop long lasting, outstanding relationships with your clients.

To me, the combination of those elements equals a happy, fulfiled life. So much is possible if you commit to working hard and adhere to the principles you'll find in this book.

The seven principles we will cover are:

- **Vision** – What do you want to achieve? Where do you want your business to go? Having a vision is integral. In this principle, we look at how to define your vision and how to align your business with your vision.

- **People** – Being in business is all about people. Your team members are the ones who help you succeed, who look after your clients and represent your company. It's so important to look after them in the first place. This principle addresses how to find the right people, how to train them properly and how to take care of them.

- **Leadership** – A strong leader is about much more than simply controlling what your company does. In this principle, we cover what you need to know about having a leadership mindset and look at how you can create a future leader within your industry by empowering others and taking less while giving more.

- **Culture** – The environment you nurture in your business makes all the difference to attract and keep the people who will make your endeavours flourish. In this principle, we will look at creating a culture of communication, idea sharing, celebration, and of course, fun!

- **Execution** – Actioning your ideas and putting processes into practice is just as important as developing your vision and overall strategy. Without proper execution, nothing can be achieved. This principle addresses how you can design efficient systems and processes, delegate departmental tasks, hold effective meetings, implement and manage processes, and award responsibility and ownership to others.

- **Marketing** – Your message is about what you want to communicate to the world and your ideal audience, through your branding and marketing efforts. This principle will help you identify your target market, articulate your message and market that message through a variety of channels. This is how people will hear about you and how you will gain industry-wide recognition for the work you do.

- **Growth** – Let's grow! This is the mindset that matters when you're looking to achieve real growth.

This chapter covers how you can take things to the next level through your people and strategy, with the support of well-sourced cash and careful execution.

★

I sat up from the floor of my office; I thought about my next move. Yes, my actions and behaviour were completely inappropriate and I felt ashamed of myself. I had hit rock bottom, but something else hit me – the realisation that I was not going to quit. *I am not a quitter!* A new day brings a fresh new start, and I wanted more than anything to begin again and build my business successfully from the ground up.

I did indeed bounce back from that night on my office floor. I want to share with you a simple message: If I can do it, anyone can do it. So read on and see how I believe your upbringing affects your business outlook and what you can do to make sure it's in the most positive way possible.

PART I

A LIFE WHICH INSPIRES PEOPLE
AND HAS A POSITIVE IMPACT
ON ITS SURROUNDINGS IS
A LIFE WORTH LIVING.

SUNIL KUMAR

MY STORY

August 25, 2004

I was a 21-year-old from Kurukshetra, a small village 180km from New Delhi, India. I was leaving the only home I'd ever known and heading for Australia in search of something bigger and brighter. My house was full of family, relatives, friends and neighbours, all wishing me well for my future. Three large cars were waiting to carry about 18 people, including me, to the airport.

As I stepped out of my house, I could see families of adults and kids from my village gathered around. When I looked up, there were people watching me from the rooftops. It was like I was going off to represent my town at the Olympic Games, with everyone having high hopes for me! One of my best friends, Pardeep, gave me a Parker pen. He knew my dreams, lofty for a boy from a small village, and the goals I had for myself at the time, as well as my ambition. He said, 'I know you will write a unique story with it – make sure it's a positive and inspiring one.' *I was ready.*

I still remember some familiar faces and their reactions from that day. It gives me pure energy whenever I think about it. I hoped someday I could do something good back home for people in need. It was a moment I'll never forget.

After a long flight, my friends in Australia came to pick me up. The drive from the airport to their place in Footscray was full of wonder as I took in the new country whizzing past the window. They lived in a house behind a restaurant, which I soon found out contained nine students, all crammed in. I would make the tenth. Within a week, we decided we needed to move and reduce numbers, so three of us found a small apartment. It was a better location, and the city views were amazing.

I was able to get a few menial jobs and I was working hard to acclimatise to the unfamiliar Australian accent. The first few months of any new situation is hard, but in an unfamiliar country with new people, few English language skills, an overwhelming shyness, my resolve was being tested. I was enrolled full-time at the Melbourne Institute of Technology, University of Ballarat, where I was studying for my English requirement as part of my condition to apply for Australian permanent residency, and was studying for my Masters of Professional Accounting at the same time.

I got my first real job: a commission-only role with Salesforce, a direct-sales company, later to be rebranded as Salmat Group. I didn't perform too well; I had limited English, and I wasn't great at selling mobile phones. My team leader eventually gave me to the company's worst performing team. I didn't blame him.

All my time was spent either working or studying. My friends and roommates were working on an hourly rate doing jobs like dish-washing, car detailing, driving taxis or 7-Eleven. They were earning consistent money, but I was on commission and hadn't earned anything in three months. I was finding life very difficult.

When I was handed over to the new team, I had two choices – sink or swim. My new team leader was happy to take me on as he didn't have many members, but he was very rude. The team members were not very happy with him; he just didn't care about them. Part of our job was door-knocking and canvassing on people's doorsteps, and he would usually drop me off in one location and ask me to knock on 50 doors. I made the decision to step things up a bit. To push a little harder than I'd been doing. I told myself I'd knock on many more doors than 50. I decided to swim.

One Saturday, we headed out to Dromana, a long way from home, and I spent the entire day knocking on doors and making no sales. My strategy hadn't worked at all. It was late afternoon, around 4.30pm, and I was tired. I sat on the footpath of a hilly area, overlooking the ocean.

I'd had nothing to eat all day and walking up and down the hilly streets had depleted my strength. I was ready to quit. The job was not improving my communication skills, nor making any money to pay my bills. If someone had walked up to me then and offered me any other job, I would have taken it.

I felt like a total failure; good for nothing. The icing on the cake was when my team leader asked me to go home by train, by myself – a three-hour journey from the Peninsula to Footscray, because I hadn't achieved any results.

DIGGING DEEP

My team leader did, however, provide one moment that really defined me. He told me something that I've never forgotten. He said, 'Sunil, the day you improve your communication you will be unbeaten, because you work harder than anyone else, and you do more than you are asked.' That day came when he had a three-week holiday, landing me the plum opportunity to work in one of the company's two best performing teams.

It was a Saturday – and I had a real sense that this was my moment to turn things around. I had a feeling the area I was going to was one where people would be more open to listening to what we had to offer. I had written and practised my scripts many times the night before and I was excited and felt ready when I was dropped into the field at about 11am. By 2pm I had made four sales! I quickly ate my snack, and went on to work every minute of the day, right up until my team came to pick me up. When everyone got in the van and the team leader asked everyone how many sales they had made, the 'top' guy had four sales. I was sitting quietly waiting for my turn as I was the new person; he skipped me, but after a few minutes, he asked me, and I said I had eight. He asked me again, and I said I had sold eight phones. He put his foot on the brake, stopped the car and started clapping for me. Then the whole team clapped, and I felt a growing sense of pride. The next week, everyone in the team came to me. I was the rookie guy that had now suddenly sold eight phones.

From there, I performed in the top three in his team and overall, in the top 10 of sales consultants, every week.

After that, Salesforce was contracted to sell to the biggest telephone company in Australia, Telstra, where I performed in the top five consultants out of 70-100 consultants working for Salesforce at the time. In 2006, I was one of the top three performers. I sold 10 landlines in one day, which is the highest amount of landline phones ever sold in one day. I won many awards weekly, monthly and yearly for best performance.

I was busy working five days a week. And I finally, happily, completed my Masters of Professional Accounting. I also qualified for my Australian dream of obtaining permanent residency, which I then received in 2007. It was great news!

Despite my shaky start, I decided to stay with the same team where I had made eight sales in a day. It was the very first uplifting culture experience I'd had, where I could have fun in an encouraging team environment and where everyone was willing to help others.

While strongly performing every day, I also helped new recruits with their training. I'd been there, in my own journey, so I had empathy with their early struggles. I helped train eight excellent new recruits, so that they could gain confidence and start succeeding in their roles. On my part, I wanted to help wherever I could. They respected me because they knew I was taking the time and going out of my way to help them, without wanting anything in return. Now, looking back, I can see that this has been my philosophy in life all along. I believe the universe gives back to you many times over.

I now felt ready to think about my next move. I could spread my wings with all the confidence I had gained from my new qualifications, where I was comfortable communicating with lawyers, taxi drivers, trades people, accountants, high-level businesspeople and executives.

At the time, I was reading a lot of biographies and self-development books and one thing was clear to me – a lot of people made their fortunes in real estate, in investing.

The house we rented in Yarraville was to be sold. When the real estate agent sold the house on auction day, straightaway, I thought – I could do that!

LAUNCHING INTO REAL ESTATE

It wasn't easy leaving my highly paid job at Salesforce to start a new career in a new industry, but I really wanted to move to the next level in my career, recognising that I needed to take a few steps back to move forward. I signed up for a real estate agent's course at Victoria University and then started applying for jobs.

Finally, I was offered one with a local agency in Altona, who was impressed with my door-to-door sales experience. As the weeks slipped by, however, I began to wonder how I could be successful as a real estate agent. So far, I was only making coffees, drinking coffees, chatting with staff over coffees, and getting to know the company and counting other's listings. As per their traditional model, I was given a desk, phone, and computer but I was expected to sort myself out; I wasn't told what to do. I decided to find a mentor.

The guy I chose was a real gun, who was hosting training in Melbourne.

He suggested lots of tools and I implemented them straight-away – listening to training audios in the car while driving to work and coming in an hour earlier to get the work done sooner were a couple of his examples. Now, I was invested to make my mark as an agent.

I knew I needed to start listing properties. So I initiated door knocks, letterbox drops and phone calls, and soon enough I had three listings. There was a $1000 bonus for listing and selling four properties a month, and I remember winning the $1000 bonus three months in row and exceeding my target every month. It came as a big surprise to the guys in my office – what was I doing to get this business? Well, I could see that none of the others were prepared to do what I was doing.

They did drops and waited for the business to come to them. They were happy for people to come to the office asking to sell their house, but they weren't prepared to head out and talk to them, making contact for future business. I stayed on top almost every month, not because I was good, but because they were not prepared to do what it took to go above and beyond like I was. It also didn't help that the agency was run by two directors who were opposites in nature and style. They disagreed with each other almost every week on several things, and after nearly three years, I felt that my time with them was drawing to an end, as I couldn't see a pathway to growth anywhere.

I started to read more about successful people in real estate and to think about opening an agency in Werribee – independently owned and operated. I had been offered a partnership opportunity before, but as I am a strong believer in learning everything before starting a business, I had always declined. But now, I was at a different stage.

RELIANCE REAL ESTATE WAS BORN

On the day I resigned from my job, I left the office with a fresh sense of newfound freedom. I was so excited to sign the new lease; our address was the first floor, 4a Bridge Street, Werribee, above the Commonwealth Bank.

I had the logo designed and started mapping out how the office would look upstairs with its green and yellow logo.

I remember the day when I first saw the office signage. I jumped with joy and did a little dance in the lift going upstairs. I was the happiest person – after all my efforts, my dream was finally coming to life.

I opened the business with my business partner and investor, who at the time shared the same vision to launch the business and start a new chapter together. We signed the lease for $65,000pa, plus outgoings, and registered with the Building Licence Authority (BLA) to carry out real estate business.

The space was an old accountant's office that went out of business, so it already had the desks, chairs, phone system, reception and a boardroom set up, across 150m² and five big rooms. We thought we'd secured a bargain!

A significant person in my life at that time was my new recruit, Ravi, a young up-and-coming man. The first time I'd met him, I had felt an immediate connection and had been looking forward to working with him. Every day for a week, the two of us went into the office before we opened. Ravi Gupta was the first person to join me, and from day one, he was a real strength. I shared most of my thoughts with him and we got along famously.

It was early 2011 – personally, I was building a house that was nearly finished and I was newly married. We were preparing for a trip to India and the USA for a couple of weeks on our honeymoon. It was a very busy time.

On May 25, we opened the office and Reliance Real Estate was officially born. We celebrated with a party at Werribee Racecourse, which featured beautiful views, great food and drinks. I made a speech, as did my business partner and investor. My family was there, and everyone wished us well for the future. What a high!

On May 26, it was day one. As there was just Ravi and I in the office, we kicked things off by cold calling and introducing ourselves to prospective clients.

We had a few listings of our own in Werribee, but our very first listing was with a client, Vaneesha, for a house on two blocks. She told us she wanted to interview a couple more agents, but we kept talking with her.

While I was doing most of the talking, I asked Ravi to pull out the authority form, and I saw that the house was listed under her name, not her husband's. He was standing next to her clearly waiting for her next move, so I looked into her eyes and said that we would bring the highest price for her property. I pushed the authority over to her to sign, and Ravi looked shocked to see me act so boldly. She stopped for a minute, looked at both of us, and said, 'Okay, I trust you to sell my greatest asset'. She signed it and it was our first exclusive listing. We were ecstatic!

In the end, we marketed her property beautifully and secured a top price after negotiating with four bidders, plus locked in a long settlement. She was happy and we created a bond with her so strong she is still one of our longest-held clients today.

THE HONEYMOON PERIOD ENDS

It was a very promising start, and those first six months were great. But we soon fell into trouble. The $90,000 overdraft from ANZ was nearly depleted and we worriedly waited for our commissions to be settled. By this stage, we had five agents, including myself, and an administration assistant.

I was managing accounts, online subscriptions, hiring, training, dealing with property, settlements, suppliers and creditors all at once. Of course, I also had an investor and partner to report to, whose values were beginning to slide quite obviously away from my own. On top of it all, I didn't make the time for prospecting, listing and selling, which was the number one thing that had made me so successful in my previous real estate career, and was my real strength. Instead, I had fallen into the trap of having so much to do managing the business that I had little time left for anything else.

Though I had always known that starting my own business would test me, working six, often seven, days a week for barely any pay started taking its toll. And then, as my team began to struggle and leave, another bombshell from my best friend, Ravi, and star agent, hit me.

We were having lunch when he told me he'd accepted another job with a higher salary, plus bonuses. I felt like a ton of bricks had fallen on me. Now, I was left with almost no money in the bank, my best performing agent had just quit, and a couple of others were not performing. This would mean that in the office it would just be me and a couple of other agents, who were still finding their feet and learning the basics of real estate.

But at least I had someone in the office who I could count on, despite wondering if he too might leave to feed his family as he wasn't making enough money to survive either.

During this time, I felt as though I was carrying a big burden. My shoulders and body were heavy, and I felt stressed both in the office and at home and I wasn't sleeping. I still tried to start my day early but waking up tired had become normal practice. Creditors were calling me as I tried to close deals, but everything was dragging. At this stage, I approached a local real estate to buy my rent roll of 24 properties. I kept working, taking each day at a time, and if I'd received a reasonable offer for the rent roll, I might never have written this book.

Furthermore, people were blaming one another for our poor performance, and I was blaming myself, questioning my ability to be a leader and grow a business from scratch. By now, I was trying to cut down running costs by downsizing on subscriptions or stopping advertising in various media sources. My business partner would ring me every second day and ask what I was going to do and if there were any commissions coming in.

FROM THE GROUND UP

Now, let me take you back to the start of the book – the day of February 23, 2013 – when I slept in the office. I was at breaking point. I knew that business owners expected to hit tough times, but this seemed almost impossible for me to handle. On the other hand, if I could sell my rent roll, I could just start over as a full-time real estate agent and enjoy a regular pay cheque.

However, I realised that I didn't want to roll over and give up. I had too much integrity, drive and determination to do that.

I had invested all my time, energy and passion into making this business work, and I didn't want to drive it into the ground.

But I also knew that it would take hard work to turn it around. It required recognising and working through the principles that I'm going to share with you. And it involved seeking answers and advice from experienced business people who had been on the same journey. Understanding the need to invest – in education, training, systems and processes as well as our people – was key.

The first step was having incredible support from my family, especially my brother and my wife. They always believed in me to make any decision about business or at home. I was very lucky to have them!

Secondly, I read a lot of books demonstrating the similar struggles of others on the same journey. By reading books like the one you are reading now, I could relate myself with them, and this inspired me to keep going on the right path.

One of the reasons I wrote this book was because during my darkest times, books about how others had overcome their struggles were a great source of inspiration to me. One that had the most impact on my thinking at the time was, *You Can Win* by Shiv Khera. Its seven steps to success formed the basis of my approach. Another was *The Australian Dream and $1 Properties* by Peter Huang. Huang arrived in Australia with next to nothing and built Yong Real Estate from the bottom up. It became the highest-ranking real estate agency in Queensland. His book is full of the wisdom that only comes from experience.

Thirdly, I went back to basics. I implemented the one sales technique I learnt in the early stages of my career. This was to make a minimum of 50 phone calls from 5-7pm every day. I knew that if I could do this, I'd sleep well at night because prospecting was my strength, and by dedicating this time to something I knew I was good at gave me comfort that I'd done my best for the day.

For the rest of the day, I cut down all non-revenue generating meetings, including media, suppliers or anything to do with online subscriptions or office equipment. By cutting out four or five meetings a week, I reclaimed six to eight hours a week, which could be dedicated to revenue generating and team building. I would ask people to send me an email with their proposal and only have face-to-face meetings if necessary.

This was the time to focus on my prospecting: meeting potential clients, listing presentations, showing to buyers and focusing on customer service and training. The rest could wait or be delegated. I focused completely on myself and my business.

And I refused to compare myself to others in the industry, or I'd get frustrated. I turned inwards and took it day-by-day, week-by-week. I was intent only on prospecting, listing and selling – *back to basics.*

As the end of 2013 approached, the first half of the year hadn't been good for us.

We were still short on money, but we'd paid most of our debts and any that were outstanding I'd promised that although they would most likely be late, I would pay them. My biggest expense was the rent, which, with just two of us in the office, was a huge outlay. So, I needed to find a cheaper solution.

In the end, our landlord agreed that we could subdivide the current office and rent it separately. This was a move in the right direction. While we still weren't making any money, I was starting to make about four sales a month which covered expenses. Then, that grew to six a month. The biggest game changer was my two hours of prospecting every day. Our sales grew to 10 a month.

We began to feel comfortable in the new space and could think about growing our team. I remember being asked by an office team member if I should throw out the business cards of my first agent, Ravi, but I said to keep them where they were. I was hopeful I could bring him back one day.

The last half of 2013 went well and 2014 even better. We started performing and agents approached us to become part of the team, bringing with them experience and energy. I continued prospecting, working hard and offering agents a supportive environment with relatively high-commission packages to come on board and work together to achieve a common goal.

The reward was three young stars, Mukesh, Sandy and Taney, who joined the business. These were the stars I'd met while at Salesforce, who had the ideal sales profile, drive and energy to turn the business around with me, by being committed, motivated and disciplined. Adding their energy to the mix gave us the performance we needed, gaining ground in a tough time.

I found out later that they'd been watching me from a distance and observing whether I was right person to lead them to a bright future. They had excellent skills, respect and faith in me, and they knew I would help them in turn become better in the long run and overall, successful.

They followed my advice without questioning it. It came as a surprise to me they were doing a lot more than what they were supposed to be doing. For example, I asked one of them to make 20-30 phone calls, five days a week, to build his clientele. He was making close to 80-100 calls a day. Within three months, our area knew there were some star performers who had joined Reliance and that they were exceptionally good at what they were doing. This was all because of my early work at Salesforce. My experience and generosity there had begun to repay me many times over.

Meanwhile, my business partner was gaining confidence that he would recover his initial investment in the business, and in the middle of 2014, we paid him out the final amounts. The day he exited the business was a huge turning point, and I could finally be free and independent. I felt light, that a huge burden was off my shoulders. I felt a great level of freedom. I was now solely responsible for all my failures and successes. I also announced to my team that we wanted to move to Werribee's Main Street.

Two weeks later, we signed a lease and moved into the new office, at 73 Watton Street, Werribee. We started the fit-out and decided to open on January 15, 2015. My whole team was full of energy for the move, and this was brilliant because it gave us a presence we didn't have before as many local homeowners had never heard of us. Already full of energy, momentum built further within the team. The business achieved record sales and the team kept on growing.

Brand recognition was also high. Instead of the early days when friends would ask our team members, 'You're working for who?', we now had new people calling us to ask when we would have a new office opening and whether there were any potential positions available. This gave me such a buzz to see what we had created together!

I have always been a people person, and I bring the same skills I learnt into my business today. I was supported as a child through good and bad times and my mother reminded me that as a child, I had always been obedient, I looked after those around me, both children and the elderly – these are qualities I continue to develop and still take pride in today. I had to reach deeply inside myself to turn my company around, and my wish is that you don't have to feel alone when it's your turn to face the fine line between giving up and keeping going in tough times.

With the right investment, tools and advice that you'll learn in the following pages, I wish for you to feel inspired by what I've been through and to continue what you have started. Do it for your own sake, for the sake of the others joining you on this journey and for the sake of the community at large.

Now, let's learn the seven principles of building a business fast!

PART II

MAKE YOUR VISION SO CLEAR THAT
YOUR FEARS BECOME IRRELEVANT.

KARWIN RAE

PRINCIPLE ONE
ESTABLISH YOUR VISION

Having a vision is really important! It can make all the difference to your success when it comes to building a business that lasts. A vision is a guide to the bright future where you want to take your business, a critical tool to steer you towards a clear purpose. A vision enables you to see what you want your business to 'be' and this can inspire you and your teams to achieve it together. It brings teams together to make them feel like a valuable part of the whole. Your business is an extension of you, and your vision for the business should extend to all areas of your life, so your personal vision should reflect your business vision. It's about what you are willing to do and become to achieve your vision.

A vision creates excitement and drives your motivation. It's the reason to get up in the morning. It's the fuel that will keep you going. Business can be hard, and this is what powers you through the tough times.

A vison creates an organised team, all focused on contributing to the future success of the business, together and united. People who are financially driven, with their only aim to make lots of money for themselves, ironically wind up making less. On the other hand, the entrepreneur who wants to create something of value, is genuinely interested in solving their clients' problems or pain points and supports their team along the way, seems to make a more positive impact and is fulfiled. These are the ones who make money along the way because money is not their only end goal, their vision for the business is their main focus. Imagine if you planted a peach tree and only focused on its fruit. You need to focus on growing a healthy tree and nurturing it. The fruit will come, but you need to follow a healthy process which is even more important than the end result.

When you don't have a vision, things may not bode as well for your company. I've seen this play out when people get one or two wins and start feeling like they've hit some kind of milestone. They can feel like it's all happening for them. But when this happens, it's easy for them to get distracted, especially in real estate. They splash out, buying luxury cars and extravagant items. This might also reflect in their commitment; they are suddenly taking longer coffee and lunch breaks and perhaps they are spending less time in the office. They are less focused on their teams and the overall 'bigger picture'. They forget the fundamentals of their daily or weekly performing routines, the things that made them successful in the first place. And as it turns out, success is very jealous of anything else you spend your time on. Without a vision, early wins can really distract you from long-term success and if you're not careful, you might wander off the path altogether and lose sight of what you really wanted your business to be.

If you don't have a vision of where you are going, you will feel disheartened by every small challenge that crops up. You'll find it harder to ride out setbacks. You might feel like everyone is against you and ask yourself – why is this happening to me? Instead, try to believe this is happening 'for' me. At times, I've been out of alignment with my vision, and I was annoyed with the challenges I faced and had become disheartened. It is my personal experience that growing a business can be difficult, unfair and harsh at times, but once you are aligned with the future you created for your business, you can handle any obstacles, understanding they are just a part of the process to reach your goals.

A strong and purposeful vision can help you see beyond everyday challenges. You have a clear direction which is aimed right ahead, and you are better equipped to move past the daily challenges and keep the end goal in mind. When things go wrong, you accept them and fix them. You value each failure for the lessons they teach you and, in the process, you become wiser every time. You embrace working hard because you know what it will mean in the long run. Your goal gives you the energy to keep pushing forward, when you might otherwise have been feeling caught up in a negative spiral.

To define your vision, take a quiet moment for yourself, away from your routine. Spend three to five days a year in a place with no distractions and minimum technology. This has been a part of my personal schedule every year since I started my business.

I travel to a remote area – I prefer to be near water or I might even choose a country town, as long as the scenery inspires and calms me. I truly give myself a break from everything. I spend quality time on my vision and analyse if I'm on the right path of my life's journey. This space is away from family and business influence so I can completely work on what I want to achieve in my life and business. In January 2016, I attended a six-day silent meditation course (yes, I was silent for six days), designed so I could learn more about myself and gain insight into my higher purpose in life. My intent was to use this time to work on the vision I had for myself and my company. Twenty-four of us woke up at 4am every day and contemplated our lives in total silence for six days. Each day included yoga and meditation, preparing vegetarian food, serving this to others, and spending time with nature away from technology or any other influence.

Towards the end, on the fifth day, we undertook a three-hour guided meditation. We achieved a very deep state of meditation, just like the instructor wanted us to discover. In this deep state, we were guided to 'see' our life coming to an end, right in front of our eyes! It was a very deep and profound experience.

We were taught to imagine we only had five days left to live. Imagine you are old and sick, dying – and you only have days left to live. It's a very confronting and eye-opening experience. If you close your eyes and imagine this, who do you see next to you, standing at your bedside? I saw my family and friends. But most unexpectedly, I also saw my team members – a team I often spend more time with than my family. In my dream state, they came to see me, to be close to me, and let me know they appreciated my influence on their lives.

Seeing my team beside me in my meditation during my dream state of the last moments of my life, changed me. I felt such a connection to them and felt the amazing impact they've had on me and I realised how incredibly important they were to myself, and to the very heart of the business. I realised that I wanted to do my best to have a positive impact on their lives, as much as my own. I also realised that if I could impact a hundred people or more through my work, my life would have been worth living. I understood that it would create a ripple effect – the hundred I helped would go forward and impact their own hundred, and then that hundred on to their own hundred. Thousands of people creating their own visions and goals for the future. This was when I truly understood for the first time the power of one person's vision.

I came to believe a small group of people really could change the world. My imagination was forever changed in the way I viewed my team and their wellbeing. I learnt it was my moral responsibility as a leader to provide them with the best platform to do their life's best work.

The meditation taught me to dream big, motivate and inspire others, and tuned me into my goal for the long term. I understood what I was learning was everything a vision should be for business, and therefore life itself.

I now wake up excited about my job every day – because I know my work has a direct impact on the personal and professional lives of my team members and their families. That makes me passionate about my future and it drives me to perform to the best of my ability every single day.

As a result, everything we have achieved has come from putting people first – our clients and our team. I believe in this so much that I've listed it straight after the vision chapter in this book, because once you have your vision, nothing else matters before you engage your team.

Spending time envisioning the long-term goal, giving detail to the vision, is worth it for the positive and unstoppable energy it generates. When you have a purpose, you never have to fake anything. Everything you do will feel authentic and radiate a genuineness to everyone who surrounds you. It's a wonderful way to feel.

You need to revisit your vision over time. A vision isn't a static idea. It's not something you decide upon, write down and never refine – it should constantly expand. You don't expect yourself to stay the same as the years advance, that you won't change, grow as a human, learn new things that take you in a different direction, so nor should you expect your business to remain unchanged. Think about the future as it could be. Don't be stuck in today's challenges. Handle them now but aim for a bigger and brighter potential. Big thinkers plan for three to five years, even ten years into the future, aligning their actions to achieve success for that time. This is important even when the present looks and feels good.

✓ **Mentor tip**

So, what is the big vision that keeps you excited every day? If you truly find what you really want and care for, you can attract a group of people to become a part of it, joining with a common interest. Once you have a vision like this, no obstacle is too big for you to overcome.

I was lucky enough to find what I love doing every day. And although I use the word 'luck' here, of course my story involves a lot more than luck. I have dedicated years of time and energy to fulfiling my vision. It's my journey of mistakes and achievements together which have shaped me and revealed my higher purpose. Now my philosophy is the more I do, the more excited I continue to be.

We all need to have a purpose for our lives. Alongside your business vision, you should consider personal, professional, health, growth, lifestyle and spiritual connection goals. For example, a parent's higher purpose may be to raise their child to be the best human being they can be, and they will do their best every day to fulfil this purpose in their life. Similarly, my purpose is to enable people and my team to fulfil their dreams and make a positive impact on them. Writing this book is part of my higher purpose, to share my story and inspire more individuals to follow the path of their own higher purpose.

Being able to express this is an excellent start to building success in business and life. But this is not always easy. If you're not sure what your passion is or what would cause you to jump out of bed in the morning, wouldn't it be great to have a process to follow to help you get there?

THE THREE STEPS

The following three steps will help you create your life and business vision. They will show you how to align everything you do with your vision by identifying the values that will bring your vision to life. They are:

1. How to create your vision

2. How to build your roadmap to achieve your vision

3. How to stay aligned to your vision.

1. HOW TO CREATE YOUR VISION

Creating your vision is about aiming towards the highest peak you could possibly reach by painting a big, dreamy picture of your future. Our vision is all about the growth and wellbeing of our people. Not just in career progression, but as better people, working in better teams, where respect and trust are shown by our behaviour, words and actions. We want to make a positive impact to enable our team to fulfil their dreams.

We also understand that if we focus on growing our team personally and professionally, the business will grow. This will provide opportunities for our team members to grow and be part of something bigger and brighter. It's exciting and encouraging, for me and for our teams too.

Everyone inside the business knows that this is what we aim for, and everyone who hears about us outside the business is aware of it, too. When we talk about growth, it's not just in terms of number of offices, size of workforce and quantity of turnover. It's the growth of our people, personally and professionally. We all want to grow and become the best version of ourselves because growth equals happiness. It's one of the key reasons people remain at an organisation.

We believe in each other and allow each other to make things happen. We consider our company a training and educational development group, which provides all the tools to enable people to fulfil their dreams. We put an enormous amount of time into the learning and development of our people, constantly designing programs and providing platforms we hope will take all of us to the next level, and beyond. An organisation will become known for its focus. I pictured our group becoming well known for providing the best training platform to train the best professionals in real estate and for providing them with bigger opportunities to grow.

A few years ago, together, we set a short-term vision to become the biggest independent real estate agency in the outer western suburbs and looked to achieve the number one agency status within 18-24 months. The impact of building towards our vision has put us in the limelight as our work has become recognised. This means greater exposure and greater opportunity to pursue further growth, for our company and our teams.

When your audience recognises you and your teams' good work, it inspires you to do more. It's how you know you're doing the right thing by your people and your wider community.

MY VISION

I'm going to lay myself bare for you now. I want to share with you my very clear purpose: what I stand for.

I want to positively influence the lives of people who come into our team and the people we touch through our products and services. With my life's work, I want to leave a positive and encouraging mark on the world around me. I'm constantly inspired to make the best use of this life. I believe it starts with my surroundings, influencing the group of people that make up my teams.

> Never doubt that a small group of thoughtful, committed citizens can change the world. Indeed, it is the only thing that ever has.
>
> Margaret Mead

I truly believe in creating the leaders of the future. They can influence their generation, leading by example. And I genuinely enjoy empowering people. That's what excites me every day. However, I won't say I had this purpose from the time I started the business. It was an internal personal attribute, but I didn't realise it until I'd been through a tough time and emerged from the other side. When three of my young and energetic team members joined my team, within six months, they were recognised for their excellent work. Between their dedication and my guidance, they were performing to the best possible level.

It gave me enormous joy to see them succeeding through that phase of their life. Since then, my aim has been to empower my team and make them see higher for themselves than they can see.

I wake up at 5:30am every morning, so I need to know why I am doing what I am doing. My higher purpose is to positively impact a large number of people through my work, create leaders to make a worthy contribution to society and even to the world at large. I'm dreaming big. I want to help others to always learn, set goals, move forward and be the best version of themselves.

Exercise

Creating a vision for life is ongoing work, but you can start with asking 'what do I want?' It is a difficult question to answer, so allow yourself to explore your deepest desire. It's good to ask some thought-provoking questions to help you discover the possibilities of what you want out of life. Give yourself permission to dream, be creative with it. You can ask yourself the questions below:

- What really matters to me?
- What am I passionate about?
- What are my dreams?

- What would bring real joy and happiness into my life?
- What are my talents?
- What would I want to accomplish?
- What legacy do I want to leave behind?

....

....

....

....

This is a great starting point to create your vision for your life and your business. As I mentioned earlier, creating, and living your vision is ongoing work. As you and your business grow, you need to keep revisiting your vision on a regular basis to align with your life's dreams and goals.

2. HOW TO BUILD A ROADMAP TO ACHIEVE YOUR VISION

It's not easy, but what you're doing is giving validation to and creating a space for your passion to live side-by-side with your work. You are the only one who can create a pathway for your passion.

You are now able to understand what you want from your life and work. But again, vision is continuous work; it will keep evolving as you grow so you should revisit your goals.

Your next step is to work backwards to see how you can achieve the future you are aiming for, and this will create the roadmap to achieving your vision.

What you'll end up with is a document of goals that you can follow step-by-step. You'll always know what you need to do next, and you'll always know you're moving in the right direction. The last step will be the best because it represents the achievement of your vision. It's a great way to map out your future success!

I believe, based on personal experience, that people who write and set goals are far more likely to achieve them than those who don't.

✓ Mentor tip

Always make sure you are in your peak state when you are writing your goals and dreams. Free your imagination and spirit to aim big and high.

Exercise

Write out the vision you have for your company and picture the ideal future you'd love to achieve. Let's break this down into milestones. Ask yourself: Where do you see yourself and your business ten years, then five years, from now? Three years from now? One year from now, and six months from now? What you do you need to learn or become to achieve your vision? What actions you need to take to achieve your vision?

It's helpful to keep a journal and continually revisit this question at regular intervals.

10 years

....

....

5 years

....

....

....

....

3 years

....

....

....

....

1 year

....

....

....

....

6 months

....

....

....

....

This approach is so valuable to every business, whether you are a fast-growing business or a small, sustainable business that doesn't necessarily want to become huge, but wants to succeed in its own space and achieve something lasting in terms of customer service and impact.

3. HOW TO STAY ALIGNED WITH YOUR VISION

Now you have part of your vision established as well as your roadmap to achieving your vision. But to fast-track your success, you need to align everything you do with your vision.

By this, I mean that *you, yourself* and your actions need to be aligned with your purpose and goal for the future. Your business is a reflection of you and everything you stand and aim for. You must focus your goals on what you love doing. If you love dealing with people, you must get involved with people in your business; if you love creating things, you must have the opportunity to engage with creativity in your business. The successful people you see are always doing something they love. They are accountable; they keep their passion and drive alive.

Basically, you must have a great interest in the field you work in. You don't want to get bored once you've been focused on your industry for just one or two years. Chances are, you're going to be doing this for a long time. So make sure you do it with great intent, energy and focus.

To stay aligned with your vision, you should always take time away from your day-to-day work, and analyse your business direction, checking if your weekly and monthly focus is aligned with your long-term vision.

There is a story about Warren Buffet that demonstrates the importance of staying focused to achieve your vision. Warren's private pilot worked for him for 10 years. He had the opportunity to ask Warren how he could achieve his goals in life. Warren, first of all, asked him to write down 25 of his life's goals and dreams, and look at what he wanted to achieve the most. After writing these down, his pilot approached him again with the list of his dreams for life. Warren asked him to circle five of the most important that he wanted to achieve. It was very hard for him to choose, but he spent some time selecting his top five. When he approached Warren again, Warren asked him if they were the top five dreams and goals in his life. He confirmed, yes, they were the most important. Warren said to the pilot, 'Promise me you will never look at the remaining 20 again, unless you achieve the top five.'

Through this story, we can learn how important it is to stay focused to achieve our dreams and goals in life. In this world of distraction, we need to have a focus to achieve our goals and vision for life.

Evaluate every opportunity against your vision and ask yourself – is it getting me closer to my goal? Ask yourself – is the attention you are giving to areas of your life the best use of your energy and focus? For me, writing this book became the same exercise for me. I evaluated the hours and days spent researching, writing and editing. I analysed this based on my vision and goals, and asked myself if it was getting me closer to my goal. The answer was a big yes every time. That's how I stayed focused on writing, despite some adverse conditions throughout my writing journey.

This is a very important step you can take to stay aligned with your vision – evaluate all your big business decisions against your vision.

EXAMPLE

When we first started, there were a few options for moving forward. We had the choice of joining a franchise group that had already established its name and one which had become quite well known. Or, we had the choice of creating something brand new, which could become a name in its own right.

There were pros and cons to both options. With a franchise, it would have been easier to get business, in the beginning. We wouldn't have to start from scratch. We could leverage the name and the reputation to attract both clients and team members. But the negative was we would have been part of someone else's identity. We would have been limited.

Most franchises don't give their team options to grow – there is hardly any recognition for individuals, and little opportunity for growth. There is no shared vision. Team members feel like they are just there to work and get paid the bare minimum. So, there is hardly any motivation for people to perform at an exceptional level. Instead, I knew that my strength lay in aligning a group of people with a common goal and creating great trust between them for long-term success.

When it came to the question of franchising, my thoughts weren't aligned and most importantly not aligned with the vision I had for the big bright future. We wanted to have the platform to empower our people, believe in them and provide them with opportunities to grow with the organisation. To do so, we had to open up the company space for them to take things forward. We realised we wanted the company to make a name for itself, and to enable our people to achieve their dreams. I knew that if I steered my team and created a shared vision, we could all achieve the extraordinary heights without limitation. It was scary, at the time, to think of being successful – it was huge, something far beyond myself – but I trusted that this was perfectly aligned with my vision and values. I spent time really envisioning the future and my vision not only for myself, but for the people who would join me on the journey. My vision brought me to clarity to start a business from scratch – that's how Reliance was born. A vision for your business and your life is invaluable. Whenever you face a decision, you can evaluate your vision to find clarity.

You are now establishing your vision. You have your purpose defined with clear goals and direction. You are working backwards and have created your roadmap to your vision.

> ✓ **Mentor tip**
>
> If you have never set out a plan to bring a bold vision to life, it's a daunting proposition. Remember to have faith in your ability and remember to trust your instincts. They have got you this far!

A business will never outgrow its leader. So this step is about recognising that your role will keep changing as the business grows. You must always learn and grow your own leadership to lead the momentum of your business. Improving your leadership is about the big changes you need to make, and capitalising on every opportunity you have by learning every day to become a better version of yourself.

On the night of the ARERA awards ceremony, when I first won Principal of the Year, I was very emotional leaving Melbourne Town Hall. It felt very pleasant walking around my city, along the Yarra River, with that trophy in my hand, taking the time to reflect and get my energy back. I stopped on the way and sat down to think about it. It was certainly one of the proudest moments of my life, hearing my name announced as winner. Ever since that day, I think to myself, how can I contribute more to my group and to the industry overall? How can I take it to the next level? How can my vision expand? How can I serve my family, my team, my community or even the wider world?

When you envision your future in a practical way, seeing it from both sides will make you more likely to be successful. At least every now and then, you must think, *What if this doesn't go right? What will happen?* This will give you more energy and power to work with – it will boost your confidence because you've thought through the scenario where you will face challenges. It will make you mentally prepared for whatever challenges you will face in pursuit of achieving your goals.

THE DANGER OF MISALIGNMENT

Achieving your vision will take all of your energy and focus, for many years. One of the major challenges is the distractions you'll experience along the way, which can easily put you off track. These distractions come in many forms. They may come as an opportunity for short-term benefit versus a more successful long-term goal, or as a distraction to your winning routine. It might be in the shape of a comparison of your journey to someone else's you've perhaps seen on social media.

Often, we come unstuck at the end because of the way we compare ourselves to other people, which can derail our carefully laid vision. This behaviour is only normal, but it can become dangerous when it's not what we want deep down and isn't aligned with our vision. We see others doing well, especially on social media, and think, *I want that for myself*, without considering the matter more deeply and delving into the why. Such ambitions do not address our emotional needs. I see a lot of people going after what other people have – they want to achieve what someone else has achieved without knowing the journey behind the achievements. But we all are different. What's good for one might not be good for another – you must seek your own truth.

EXAMPLE

In late 2017, I was published on the front page of the local newspaper. We opened three new offices and were recognised as one of the fastest growing companies in the country. I was so happy, because this had been my desire for a long time. It related to materialist desires like being famous and the idea that people would know me.

But that triumphant feeling was short-lived; I was over this excitement within a couple of days. From that experience, I realised that I do not want to work on anything which had only materialistic achievements or which did not align with the vision and purpose I had set for myself and my company. I believe long-lasting happiness comes with ongoing value, loving what you are doing daily and keeping your priorities right and seeing the positive impact on the lives of others around you.

Summary

- Consider your vision in business and come up with a big dream, purpose or long-term goal; a bright future of where you want to take your business. Truly see into the future of what you want your business to 'be' and inspire yourself and your teams to reach a shared vision.

- Once you have a picture of what you want, work backwards so you can see how to achieve it. Come up with milestones and a roadmap with markers along the path that show you that you're mastering your goals step-by-step and staying on track.

- Check that you are aligned with your vision and that what you want to achieve truly matters to you – that it is something that will truly fulfil you. Align everything you do with your vision by identifying the values to live by and work for every situation.

- Envision what is to come and picture your future successes and challenges. Be prepared but don't feel like you need to know everything. A vision is there to motivate you, so you keep moving forward.

COMPANY CULTURE IS THE BACKBONE
OF ANY SUCCESSFUL ORGANISATION.

GARY VAYNERCHUK

PRINCIPLE TWO
TAKE CARE OF YOUR PEOPLE

You might have the latest technology, the best equipment, the most professionally written vision and the strategy to go with it, but if you don't have the right people, you won't have a good business. It's really that simple. Business is all about people, and people are key to success for your organisation.

One of our leaders once told me that it's hard to find and retain good people to build a team. I replied that people are the hardest part of business – if you do not have the right people in the right seats doing the right jobs, you'll never be able to reach anywhere near your business's full potential.

People who are the right fit for your organisation will do better in their jobs and will be happier within your business, culture, team and environment. Sure, everyone will be different – every person is unique – but the right people will contribute to building a well-rounded team. Some people will be happy to stay in one role while others will want to grow and take on bigger roles and responsibilities. You'll find that there's a mix, and that could be challenging at times, but it can be wonderful.

In this chapter I'll outline how you can make this happen for your business. We'll break it up into two key sections, including several examples and exercises:

1. Finding people who are aligned with your vision
2. How to give your team the right environment for their long-term success.

To kick things off, I want to share with you one of my favourite examples to illustrate this principle, so you can see how far you can go to get the right team members in place.

It was January 2015, a year before I undertook my meditation course. Business was good. We had relocated to Main Street in Werribee, and there was a great vibe in the team and positive responses coming in from clients. I felt we were ready for another step: opening an office in our neighbouring suburb of Point Cook. I believed this was a fantastic strategy to gain market share and grow the business.

In this early growth stage, I needed to choose a person to lead the new office. I had the perfect candidate in mind. You may remember Ravi from 'My story', who followed me into the new business I was launching. He was working five days a week and enjoying his weekends. We were still good friends and I always had it in my mind to bring him back to real estate one day.

While we started planning and researching the market, I went to see Ravi's family, who were visiting him for three months. I touched on the idea of embarking on a new business venture, only planting a seed with his family. At that time, Ravi didn't know anything about us opening a new office or the fact we were considering him to lead that office.

Over a few weeks, I presented Ravi with my plans. I needed to give him an offer he couldn't refuse. I was prepared to invest significantly to set up the office, while still giving him partnership in the office. When I presented this to him, he couldn't believe it. His main question was, why him?

This was the million-dollar question. I could only answer that I couldn't think of anybody else more capable to run the office successfully. I believed in him. I knew he was very disciplined, with excellent people skills and just a really good and honest person. He would be the perfect leader for this office. I knew I had to have the right people in the right places to make this business endeavour work and the right person to make it happen.

Of course, he was fearful about coming back and worried about the idea of failure. But he took the advice I always follow – to do it anyway.

The rest is history. We opened the office in Point Cook and within the first eighteen months we were one of the top three agencies running in that area. It added huge credibility to our brand. Bringing back my original colleague and friend was a massive part of making that happen. I had pursued him relentlessly, and it worked, which illustrates what you need to do sometimes to get the right team around you.

> ✓ **Mentor tip**
>
> Always be prepared to put in the hard yards to recruit the best team around you. Whether you're attracting someone you know or don't, it's important to just go for it. Research who you are interested in, have in-depth conversations about who they are and what they are looking for. Don't be afraid if you come off looking a little silly. It's worth it.

1. PEOPLE WHO ARE ALIGNED WITH YOUR VISION

With my example above in mind, let's return to how you know what to look for when looking for a new team member. Get this right, put people first, and you'll fast track your business's success. As I mentioned before, everything we have achieved in our business is because we find and train the right people. It is fundamental to everything we stand for and do.

But you do need to know what to look for, and this can be hard, especially when you may only have a resume in front of you and a face-to-face interview upon which to base your decision.

That's why when we come to recruit our team members, we look for five key factors. They are skills and attributes we identify in our existing high performers.

Over the years we have seen some personality traits common in high achievers and we developed five criteria for our ideal candidate profile.

I. ENERGETIC AND DRIVEN

It's not always about the skills. A person with the 'right' energy and positive attitude can be more important and valuable to the team. Regardless of a person's role in the business, whether it's out selling on the front line, in a leadership role, or in the 'engine room' performing an administrative role, creating success takes incredible energy. People who have an amazing positive attitude, with the right drive to succeed, are more likely to perform well and move up within the business.

You will know when you're face to face – you'll get a sense of their energy. That's why I prefer the face-to-face interview. Of course, this isn't always possible with potential travel restrictions, so the online option is always a back-up. Essentially, we're after an energetic line-up of team players who are motivated and driven to take responsibility and drive things forward, so whether in person or online, try to truly connect with the essence of who the potential candidates are and what they will bring to the table.

II. ACHIEVERS

From experience, we find that former athletes and high achievers in their previous roles or schooling work out well in our business because of their dedication, discipline and drive. They already have the right mindset, because it has been an important part of the way they have played their sport or found success previously. These skills are directly transferable into business. We focus on hiring an 'achiever' and providing them with the right training and guidance, as it's likely they will shine and demonstrate strong achievements quickly. Therefore, we will grow much faster.

When hiring, you not only need to look at someone's resume to see what they have achieved, you could verbally ask them about something they have been successful at and are most proud of in their life.

III. TEAM PLAYERS

We can only achieve great things in sport or business with a good team of people. In business, you need great team players to build a winning culture and a healthy environment for everyone to excel. We value team players so highly that even if we find someone who is a superstar, we may not hire them if we think they're not a team player.

A good example is the All Blacks rugby team. They're the number one sporting brand in the world, and they pride themselves on being team players. There are no egos and they eschew a firm 'no dickheads policy', which means that no one is too 'big' to sweep up after themselves after a game. As per their famous motto, 'Sweep the Shed', the players are taught not to believe they are too big to do what needs to be done and are subsequently given the responsibility of being team players. It's an excellent philosophy and one I think all business leaders need to implement this mindset.

IV. VALUE ALIGNED

It is important to hire people who are aligned with your team values. One of the key values we teach in our business is to strive to become one of the best professionals we can possibly be. A great way to judge if your potential new team member is aligned with your team values is to check out how they performed in their previous roles. A person who is aligned will find great comfort within your existing team. If you hire based on your core team values, not only will your new recruit find a home in your organisation, but your existing team members will feel empowered, and every team member will then be working towards the same goals and outcomes. It is a lot more fun, and you'll all have greater success, if you work with value aligned people.

V. LOCAL RESIDENTS

Supporting the local community is very important. It's an excellent idea to employ a local as they know the streets, amenities, surroundings and local contacts. Local for us means they live in the western suburbs, rather than someone who needs to drive an hour and a half to and from work. A candidate has to be exceptionally good for us to go outside the local area. Most of our team members live within 30 minutes from work. It mainly applies to the sales team, however – this means when they receive a buyer or vendor call, they can be available within 30 minutes. Sometimes that plays a key role when a buyer wants to see a property for the final time before making an offer.

DINNER TABLE TEST

Finding the right person to fit into your business is not always about what you see on paper.

The dinner table test is the easiest way to consider someone for a role in your business. After a 15-30 minutes discussion with this person, ask yourself if you're happy to have dinner with them and share your goals and thoughts. It seems easy, but it's a hard test. If you think someone has good quality attributes, you'll invite them for dinner. If not, do you really want them representing your clients' greatest asset?

Integrity is an important factor in building success and it's one of the main criteria we seek in a team member. In the interview process, you can ask them how long they've stayed in previous jobs and look at their history to see if they have changed jobs frequently. This can give you a good indication of how stable they've been and provides an opportunity to ask them about it if they've stayed short-term in a number of positions. Someone who acts with integrity always stands by their word and wants to be reliable. And that's the person you want to hire in your business. You could also listen to any negative words – a team member who is negative towards their current or past company may not be a positive team member. When dealing with our client's greatest asset, it becomes vital we recruit the best people.

WHAT'S NOT SO IMPORTANT

Experience in the industry can certainly prove valuable, but we prefer to take someone onboard with no real estate experience as long as they come with other qualities. Some of the successful people we've hired have come from direct sales, customer service and hospitality. But if they're a high achiever with strong people skills and a positive life philosophy, that's what matters. Once we put the right person through their training and show them the pathway to success, they will most likely succeed.

Meanwhile, the ideal attributes will not only differ from business to business but also department to department.

For example, the person who sits front of office in any of our locations has to be smiley and friendly with high energy, someone who is kind and naturally helpful. We want this person to create a welcoming environment and help drive the energy of the rest of the office. This is crucial when greeting our customers and supporting our team.

✓ Mentor tip

You don't want every team member to be a clone of you, or a set of people who are all the same as one another, but you do want people who share a set of traits and have the capacity to embrace a common mindset. This list of attributes and focus on our values (see the previous Principle) helps us find the right people.

This is something you can do, too, so that you can choose people to help you grow together and achieve a shared vision.

Exercise

Think about the traits you would like in someone who is going to be a part of your organisation. What are the key attributes they should have? What aspects will ensure they fit into the workplace culture? What qualities will make them good at their job? What characteristics will enable them to play a part in helping the business achieve its vision?

Now, think about the people you already employ who do a stellar job. What is it about them that makes them so brilliant?

Think about the people you employ who are more lacklustre, less high performing. What is it about them that holds them back?

Do they lack any defining features? Is it that they need more training – which you can provide – or is the will to work just not there, regardless of the opportunities you offer them?

With all of this in mind, list five attributes and criteria that a team member absolutely must meet to be a good fit in your business and perform well in their role.

1. ....

2. ....

3. ....

4. ....

5. ....

Now, let's take this to the next level and develop your ideal candidate profile. The process of getting specific will help you recognise the people you're looking for when you start going through applicants. You can keep going with this and go into as much detail as you like.

Paint a colourful and precise picture of the perfect candidate and delve a bit deeper and ask yourself *why* these things are important to you.

Ask yourself and write below:

- What are the qualities and attributes in your perfect team member like?
- How old are they?
- Where are they from / where do they live?
- Do they speak other languages?
- What do they value?
- Why do they want to work with you?
- What are their goals in life?
- What motivates them / what lies beneath?
- What do they list as their greatest achievements?

....

....

....

....

....

....

....

....

....

....

2. HOW TO GIVE YOUR TEAM THE RIGHT ENVIRONMENT FOR THEIR LONG-TERM SUCCESS

If you recall the end of the introduction, I was in a dark place. It was 2012 and I was trying to pick myself up off the floor – physically and mentally. My business partner had walked out, and I was really struggling with the business. Each day was a challenge both professionally and personally, and even though I had been prepared for things to be tough, I was finding it hard to handle all the difficulties.

At times like these it's challenging to prioritise learning opportunities – as you're very busy just trying to stay afloat and all your energy is going into that. But I took the time to attend Tony Robbins's business mastery course, based in Fiji, for one week. I was spending money that many would have said I couldn't afford to spend, but I saw it as an investment.

Rather than continuing to do the same things day by day and hoping for a miracle to come out of thin air and change things, I had to learn how to do things differently and be my own miracle-maker.

I came back encouraged and motivated to see beyond the current challenges to what lay beyond. I also worked on my routine to get the best out of my days. The most significant change I made to my routine was implementing a run first thing in the morning. This gave me so much energy to get through a tough day and to make the most out of every day.

Regardless of the stage of my business, having a teacher and learning from others who have achieved greater success, has always been an integral part of my progress. I regularly study great business and sports people; those who have great coaches and mentors who have guided them to focus on the most important areas of their professions and helped them to perform at their best.

Sachin Tendulkar, former international cricketer regarded by many as one of the best batsmen in cricket, kept on improving his game right up to his retirement. And this was even when – especially when – no one could even come close to his success rate. Another great that comes to mind, and someone who works harder than anyone else, is tennis superstar Roger Federer, who has won 20 Grand Slam titles and continues to practise and train to improve his game.

Steve Jobs, American business magnate, was a pioneer of the personal computer innovation and in 1976 co-founded Apple, one of the most highly successful, mass-produced computers. Among many other ground-breaking triumphs, he also created the company Pixar, which produced the first 3D computer animated feature film *Toy Story* (1995), before going on to make over 20 films in one of the most successful animation studios.

The most successful sports stars work hard with the mindset that they can always improve their game. Former All Black Brad Thorn's mantra, 'Champions Do Extra', made him one of the most successful players in rugby history. His philosophy was simply finding ways to do more – in the gym, on the field or for the team.

Continuous improvement and creating an ongoing learning environment, no matter how successful you are, is at the very core of any successful sports person, business person and professional. So for me, learning from others and improving my game is the standard I set for myself and always live by.

✓ Mentor tip

Remember that your standard is set by your least trained people – not your best people, as you might think. If my best agent goes out there and does a great job presenting to a client, that's great. But if someone ill-trained goes out there and gives a client a bad impression, they get a bad impression of the whole company.

There must be a minimum standard your teams work to – a level they can perform at, so your customers only ever receive the best care and receive the best service.

If they're not shown what to do, they can harm the culture and give clients bad experiences. But if they don't receive good training, that's not their fault – it's yours. It's up to you to prioritise training to provide a great start and a continuous improving environment for your team. You are responsible for providing the right training environment for success. It is very sad to see many new recruits both in real estate and in other industries leave with a bad taste not because they weren't good at their jobs, but because they were not given the right training to be successful in their chosen career.

Why are some individuals and organisations more successful than others? Well, the best ones think and act effectively by continuously investing in people.

As a business leader, it's your job to keep your people happy in your company, and this is where your business must be adequately structured to provide what they need. After years of recruiting and retaining some of the best talent in the industry, I have learnt that it's not only about providing one particular magical thing, but also a combination of three main provisions:

i. training

ii. remuneration

iii. recognition

I. TRAINING

Master the training of your organisation, and your team will want to learn and grow with you. Training is the most important part of any growing organisation, creating high-performing companies, high retention and the opportunity for star performers to shine. Training is how you upgrade your team talent and move onwards to generate business success.

Good training starts from the top. If you, as the leader, create your business as a learning and educational organisation to strive to become the best version of yourself, your team will naturally follow. That's why training and development should never be treated as a box to tick, to look good in front of clients. Your team members will see through this and you'll start seeing higher numbers not performing to their fullest potential and this will result in team members leaving to find a better work environment. If you are not looking to train yourself, it'll rarely work asking it of your team.

It's important to remember that training is not a one-size-fits-all solution. Everyone is different, and everyone learns differently. Some prefer achieving top results working autonomously, while others thrive in a team environment. New team members will enter each business with different mindsets and different experiences. This is especially true when hiring new recruits where you have the opportunity to set them on the right path from the beginning. Good training helps the team adopt your culture and become comfortable as well as confident in their new roles.

For example, by mid-2015 things were moving along well in our business. We had two offices and a team of 24.

The team was young and energetic, but I felt we needed some expert external guidance to help us move to the next level. As a result, I attended a real estate conference on Hamilton Island, Queensland, called the Business of Real Estate.

The conference was a game changer for our business. From there we engaged the RER network as our official training and development partner. Not only did it help the team up-skill and grow in confidence, but it also removed a lot of the burden from management and provided a better pathway for the team to utilise their full potential. Today, we remain a committed part of the RER organisation, and it is our prime source of training and development.

Michael Sheargold has become my business mentor and RER has been our secret advantage, providing an excellent pathway for us to succeed to higher levels. I strongly believe we hired the best in the business to become the best in the business.

As you can see, training is exalted within our business. It is an integrated part of our business but everyone attends more than willingly. They know great training is an investment not just in the future of the business but also in their own personal and professional success. After all, knowledge is wisdom. And wisdom breeds success. It all starts with you – the leader of the organisation.

What's the best training to implement?

Now that you have recruited your team and have committed to ongoing training, you need to implement the things you've learned. You can listen and make notes, but it's by putting things into action that you can go beyond receiving education and achieving your goals.

In our business, we have actioned a series of training and development programs which offers excellent opportunities for our team to learn and grow. From the beginning we treated Reliance as an educational and development organisation. Our aim has always been to provide our team with a professional, uplifting environment to enable each person to grow. Part of our vision includes the idea that when an individual grows, the whole organisation grows.

These include:

- Onboarding process – in our company, education starts from day one. Everyone receives a welcome pack and goes through a four-week onboarding process when they join the business. They learn about the company history, vision, mission, values, and most importantly, how to excel at their job.

- Specific training manuals – to ensure our teams are trained properly, we have training manuals tailored to different job descriptions. These manuals aren't very lengthy, deeply technical or go into a high level of detail but presenting people with a guide starts them off on the right foot.

- One-on-one training sessions – with the leadership team and sales team. This session is considered one of the most important. Undertaken monthly it can be tailored to individual needs. Many times, we find that if someone within the organisation is doing an excellent job in a specific area like customer service, prospecting, listing, vendor care, buyer or landlord care, those individuals can provide training to other team members.

- Quarterly training – Our quarterly training is mainly based on the current quarterly theme of the business. Often it will revolve around excellent customer service. We select one specific area and direct our focus. Our coaching and training partner, RER Network, holds these sessions quarterly.

- We encourage our team to attend online or in-person courses to up-skill and hold sessions so that team members with specific skills can share them and foster similar skills within others throughout the group.

- We train our people to follow our client and team core values. For example, our client core values are to put the client first. It is an excellent training tool. We train the teams on real life examples on how to keep the clients' interest at all times.

- We hold annual training sessions at the beginning of each year where we host a full day of training and coaching. The entire focus is motivation and we share success stories from outside our profession. We also focus on achieving excellent results in real estate and how to achieve personal and professional goals for the coming year.

Exercise

Think about how influential your business is to your team members. What do new team members learn when they join – and what do they learn on an ongoing basis?

....

....

....

....

....

....

....

Think of the training and education you've received in your career. What stood out for you? What lessons have you taken onboard and implemented? Also look around within your industry, and even beyond, at how other high performing companies are training their teams.

....

....

....

....

....

....

....

....

Finally, bring it all together by thinking of five key things you want your teams to know and to receive training on. You can also involve your teams in brainstorming sessions to see what it is they would like to learn or need extra training in to perform at the best level possible.

1. ....

2. ....

3. ....

4. ....

5. ....

Note down what they have suggested for their own growth, improvement and success and use these tools to create your own continuous training from their feedback.

II. REMUNERATION

It's fair to reward more to the people who work hard, who have better experience, who are aligned with your team values and add more to the team in general. In our business, we generally have a very generous remuneration, slightly above the market. The structure used to be standard with the rest of the industry, but we changed in our early years to a slightly higher pay structure to retain and keep rewarding brilliant team members.

Now, even the new recruits begin with a highly reasonable pay structure to have the best start possible. This means they can focus their energy at work on producing the best results because they feel valued and rewarded. For those exceptional performers who add enormous value through their work it is only logical to offer extras when they are providing a higher contribution to success themselves.

Everyone is more satisfied knowing they are rewarded on the higher side for their dedication and hard work. As I believe in giving a better or bigger half, I've found that this structure pays off over and over in the long term in business, as well as in life. In this way, you will build a dedicated group of loyal and hard-working team members who feel they are very well looked after, and who can contribute in a major way to the culture and happy workplace with a higher level of productivity. In the long run, it pays off many times over to reward your team.

III. RECOGNITION

It's our basic human nature to seek appreciation for the things that we do. In our work, it can really lift our approach when everyone across the business receives some form of recognition. In our business, we hold recognition and yearly awards. When we held them for the first time, magic happened. We had various categories to recognise the different levels of performance. Our best team members were celebrated and the whole company acknowledged the high performers in the team, encouraging the rest of the team to perform better as well. One of the best things to come out of these recognitions was that everyone worked hard to prove themselves and wanted to stay on top and become a high performer.

At both of our awards programs, we don't just recognise the top performers in sales, but we award team members from other departments, such as front office and coordinators, to perform at their best. An example is our Team Player of the Quarter, which is about rewarding the person who contributes more to the team and is ready to help others; nothing to do with sales performance. The benefit is that it encourages individuals to play as a team – one of our core values – and in the process makes for a fun working environment for all. We recognise people on the basis of our core values to keep our values prioritised. Of course, these awards are a vehicle to encourage our team to step forward and inspire those future leaders to take an active role in the business.

However, recognition doesn't have to be about big achievements all the time. It can also be an appreciation for good work verbally, or a small reward in the form of a dinner voucher for successfully completing a task. If you start with an appreciation culture and are appreciative of good work, this good work will flow through the organisation to all your team members. Sometimes, offering a genuine acknowledgement can be as valuable as presenting awards, such as thanking the office coordinator for keeping the office in order and providing a welcoming feel for all visitors. It's important to notice things like this when they happen – it's worth a lot. I always try to seek genuine reasons to appreciate my team. It all starts with you. Think of ways you can recognise your teams in any form or shape. We have a saying in our business – catch people doing things right.

TAKE EXTRA CARE OF YOUR PEOPLE

If you don't look after your people, it's more likely that they will start to look elsewhere for work. And it's probably no surprise to you that this happens very commonly within the property industry. There's no doubt about it, bricks and mortar are a high turnover profession. The industry average is that only 20-30% of people stay in residential real estate more than one or two years from their starting time.

In our group, our retention rate is well above 80%. I am so proud and humbled by this number, because it means we are doing things right. Because we find the right people, first, and then have excellent training and education programs, chances are that the people we hire stay for the long term. And that's brilliant for business.

Once you have the right people in *your* business, how do you keep them? How do you take care of them and ensure you are nurturing them so they can achieve their potential?

As we've outlined, money and recognition can only go so far. Some companies make the mistake of always chasing new team members, offering them extra incentives, rather than looking after their existing team and creating loyal, long-term relationships. Furthermore, a lot of companies focus on the hiring process and getting new people at the expense of nurturing the ones who are already there. Just because they've proven that they can do their jobs, doesn't mean they should then be left alone and expected just to get on with it.

Instead, think long-term and be prepared to get personal. At a business level, performance goes up when the team knows that you care and have their best interests at heart. When they have that awareness, it also makes it easier for them to come to you with any challenges. This means you really have a finger on the pulse of what's going on in your organisation, rather than being met with surprises.

THE VALUE OF THE 'ONE-ON-ONE'

In our business, we take the time to understand our team members – not just pay them to carry out instructions. So, as well as your other initiatives, I strongly recommend having a one-on-one (an informal face-to-face conversation meeting) with each team member at least once a month.

The one-on-one is about checking in to see if they are facing any challenges at work or even in their personal life. You'll probably find one of your team members is not performing well or is not doing what he or she is supposed to be doing. Eight times out of ten, you'll find something that is bothering them.

Start with the location for your one-on-one. A cafe or restaurant which has a nice ambience would be the best location for a one-on-one meeting. You and the team member are away from the daily working environment and will have the best chance to open up about any challenge they might be facing at work, or even in their personal life. If you can get to the root of the problem, you can tackle the issue and make it easier for everyone concerned.

Even if it's just for 30 minutes, and even if it's not work-related, it's important to check up. If you can reassure them your discussion is confidential, they will feel more comfortable sharing with you.

As a leader, when you go out of your way to empathise with your people, you're showing them that you genuinely care. It will have a direct impact on their wellbeing and as a result they will perform better.

Often when I have a one-on-one, I receive a message afterwards saying something like, 'Thank you so much for coming up to me. I really appreciate your time.' The team member's work generally improves. Everyone wants to feel acknowledged and appreciated – like an individual. And you have the power to make that happen. The one-on-one connection you build with your team goes a long way.

SHARING VISION AND VALUES WITH YOUR WIDER TEAM

I was always reluctant in sharing our vision and goals with the whole team.

The very first time I shared my vision in full detail was in early 2015. I really opened up to the long-term plan of what we were working on behind the scenes, which was to empower and equip our teams to achieve a better career and greater influence. Our clients and the people in our teams have always been top priority. Understanding the importance of sharing the vision led me to let my team know the details and steps we were taking behind the scenes to enable the team to fulfil their own dreams and our vision of becoming one of the top three agents in any market we serve.

Our core values show how we wish to behave and what we'd like to be known for in the market. By sharing these and by living by our purpose, vision and core values, team moral and engagement went to the next level. But most importantly the whole team was aligned to move in the same direction.

Even if you do not have a big vision to share, it is still important to have collective talks with your whole team to discuss core values, behaviour and key principles for them to continue to improve their excellent performance.

GET THE TEAM INVOLVED IN KEY DECISION AND PLANNING

There's no magic trick to keep your team happy, encouraged, engaged and aligned.

Over the years, we've tried various tools and techniques like the one-on-one, as we believe that it's crucial to also engage your wider team to feel valued and therefore deliver success for the business.

It has been my philosophy that getting the right people involved in decision-making at an early stage gives them a sense of belonging, and most importantly, it gives me a different opinion or perspective on the matter. Team members also feel validated. One of the ways we demonstrate this is by holding wider team meetings. One of the main events in our calendar is the Strategy and Planning Day.

Every year around November, we hold the planning session with our key team members. In November 2020, 24 of us attended the one-and-a-half day, overnight event with one whole day devoted to the strategy session. We reviewed what was working well, what challenges we were facing and the key projects we aimed to be involved with in the coming year. By the end of the day, we had a great list of items to take away with us; we had a solid idea of what we needed to improve for the business, as well as an excellent understanding of the current and upcoming challenges. We designed the next year's project priorities with some quick wins, put together our quarterly themes, then workshopped which items would be relegated to the second half of the following year.

Holding an annual key planning and strategy day with selected performers and leaders in the business provides opportunities for team members to create change in the business, to see and appreciate what is being done now, as well as gives them a voice in the direction and success of the business.

We also encourage our people to 'take ownership of their area.' We give people their work and show them how to do it, but in return we ensure they understand that they then take ownership of what they are doing.

✓ Mentor tip

The bigger your company, the harder it can be to see each and every person yourself. But you can put structures in place so that the leadership team always reaches out and no one gets forgotten or overlooked. This means, you can potentially help with their challenges or put support in place for them. Beyond that, you have created a bond between you that you can build on for the future.

Exercise

Take the time to consider your existing team members. What management structures are in place? What are you doing to check in with them now?

....

....

....

....

....

Do you think your teams are well looked after? Is there anything further you could do to ensure their voices are heard? How can you empower your teams?

....

....

....

....

....

Summary

- Your people are your business. To thrive as an organisation, you not only need to find the right people, but also take good care of them.

- We've developed our top five attributes to ensure we are on track to find the best team:

  1. energetic and driven
  2. achiever
  3. team player
  4. value aligned
  5. local residents.

- What does your team need from you? The top three factors are:

  1. training
  2. remuneration
  3. recognition

- Invest in training and education – for yourself and for every member of the team. Have an onboarding process that welcomes them into your culture and makes them comfortable as well as confident about doing their job.

- Provide training on an ongoing basis and encourage the team to implement the learning, not just to listen and take notes.

- Making people feel appreciated doesn't always have to be as big as rewards and formal recognition, though these things are great. It can be as small (and valuable) as offering praise about anything that shows you notice the contribution your team makes. These are the people who make your business everything it is and everything it can be in the future. Catching people doing the right things and acknowledging them has a positive impact on everyone.

- To keep your team happy, take care of them. Speak with them as individuals, one-on-one, at regular intervals, so you can come to understand them. Support them and help them achieve their potential. Acknowledge them, appreciate them, and show them their opinion matters. Give them the praise they deserve and empower them.

A LEADER IS ONE WHO KNOWS THE WAY,
GOES THE WAY, AND SHOWS THE WAY.

JOHN MAXWELL

PRINCIPLE THREE
A TRUE LEADER

Now we are really cooking, for leadership is one of my favourite topics. I want to share this important fact with you: *everything is a skill.* Even happiness is a skill; you can develop the skill of being happy despite your circumstances. The more you think about it, the more you will see the possibility of acquiring all the skills you need. No one is born a leader, athlete, scientist, doctor or entrepreneur.

In business, many people think leadership is a talent that is gifted to only a select few, but in fact it's a skill that can be developed like any other skill. One of the key traits of leadership is appreciating your team and encouraging them to be the best version of themselves. It is purely a skill of appreciation, which can be developed by being real and authentic, reading books on leadership, appreciating great work or attending seminars on leadership.

When I first started the business, I fell into the trap of having too much to do *managing* the business. I was managing accounts, property, HR, settlements, subscriptions, suppliers, and creditors all at once. I was working hard in and on the business; busy hiring and firing, building and training a team, developing plans and delivering on the promises made to my team and clients. I was the answer to anything and everything in the business. Basically, I was doing a lot of managing. But I wasn't left with the time and energy to properly *lead* the business forward.

A wise leader delegates tasks and assigns others ownership of different areas so that they are free to build the future for these teams and the company. They hand over responsibility, creating trust, ownership and accountability. They can't lose themselves doing everything across every department. They lead by creating more leaders around them. This is something we'll visit in more detail in the later chapter on execution.

✓ Mentor tip

There is so much more to being a true leader than being in control and directing operations. It's not just about being the one who makes decisions and tells people what to do. It's about getting your hands dirty in the business and showing that you work as hard as any team member.

Being a leader involves a huge amount of responsibility, because now you must do your job brilliantly at the same time as being responsible for the success of your team. The best way forward is to lead by example. If you're leading by example in every area of your role, almost 60% of your job as leader is done.

If you want to grow and become the fastest growing company in the country, you need to create leaders around you who can take on bigger tasks. My primary job is to locate them, empower them, believe in them and constantly lead them in the right direction. The moment you feel they are ready or near ready, you can give them a small leadership task to test their ability.

EXAMPLE

This is exactly what we did with one of our top performers, Sandy Rana. He was doing a great job in his field, becoming the top performing agent in his market within 12 months of working in real estate.

To enhance his leadership skills before we put him in charge of opening a new office, we appointed two new team members to train under his supervision. He was responsible for their success – and at the same time had to maintain his performance as a leading agent. That would be the proof of leadership.

Sandy did a fantastic job leading the new team members and trained them to become exceptional and productive at their job. At that point, we knew he was ready to lead an excellent team of people. When our third office opened in Melton under his leadership, it became number one within 12 to 18 months. I now have very little need to work on this office as we have an excellent leader guiding an entire team of very talented people.

If you can't create more leaders, it will be hard to scale your business.

In this chapter, we're going to look at different ways to help you become a better leader. There are seven proven methods that worked brilliantly for us and I hope they work for you:

1. own your mornings
2. keep the end in mind
3. be naïve
4. empower others
5. act fast
6. take less and give more
7. take nothing personally.

These are all practical, and all achievable. Let's unpack what it takes to become a great leader together, and you'll be able to bring these into your own work. There is more to leadership than meets the eye. It's an ongoing process, always learning and growing, but ultimately one that is immensely satisfying when everything aligns.

1. OWN YOUR MORNINGS

Over the years I have studied some of the best leaders in the world and attended many seminars on leadership. There are a lot of good TED Talks and podcasts on leadership available, particularly focusing on morning routines. One thing is crystal clear; most leaders or high performers in any field are early risers.

Each morning I spend mostly silent, dedicating all my energy to the start of the day, making important decisions and getting as much as I can done in those precious hours.

I have always been a morning person, but a real shift happened when I read and began to follow the guidance of Robin Sharma's *The 5am Club*, which is an absolute masterpiece. The biggest takeaway was to wake up at 5:30am every morning and spend one hour exercising, reading, writing or whatever it is you enjoy.

I spend about twenty minutes of the first hour reading and learning, then twenty to thirty minutes exercising, either running, yoga and meditation, going to the gym or walking.

This prepares me mentally for the rest of the day as I'm always full of energy and focused on getting the best out of the day. It has been an absolute game changer for me!

One of the amazing things that has happened since starting this routine is that I do not procrastinate any more. I know clearly what I want from my day, every day, and my communication is very clear with my team. We hold ourselves back every time we don't make a decision, or even when we do plan but don't stick by it. As a leader, you need to be sure where you are heading, so the whole team understands the correct direction. Consistency in your routine and high energy is the key to long-term success.

Basically, the way you start each day has a massive effect. I recommend you come up with a morning routine for yourself that works for you – and get up early enough to get it done. I promise it will fill you with energy and clarity.

But let's face it; some of us are simply not morning people. If you're more of a night owl, chances are you're going to find it extremely difficult to get up earlier. I recommend having a timely start to the day even if you are a night person. Set a time every day where you wake up and start your day full of energy. If you're like me, it could be 5.30am. But it could also be anywhere between 6am to 7am. The key is to keep it consistent, which will keep the energy high. The best thing about mornings is that you give the best energy to the most important tasks of the day.

Getting to the office by at least 7:50am gives me dedicated and uninterrupted time to stay focused and get important work done. I often get more done in those morning hours than in the rest of the day. A lot of us naturally have more energy, drive and clarity in the morning hours, so utilise this in your favour. I also leave some decision-making for the early hours as this can be a better decision-making time of the day.

Most of the top leaders in business, sports or in life are early risers. They want to devote the best energy to the most important task of the day. If you are a morning person, it will be easy for you with some preparation to have an easy and productive start. But if you are a night person, like a few of my team members, I suggest you still set a fixed time to wake up and set your routine to get the most out of the start of the day. Be consistent with your mornings.

2. THE END IN MIND

It may seem counterintuitive to start with the end in mind but stay with me. Think about your vision or goals you want to achieve by a certain date and work backwards from there.

As I wrote about earlier, an important part of this is to have your goals and a written plan to achieve them. In other words, it's a lot harder to achieve success if you don't know what you're aiming for. So, aim high and give yourself the tools to get there with a proper written plan.

In doing so, every action you take will be attuned to that end goal. With no interruption or disruption, every decision can be made with greater clarity. Importantly you will be able to say no to the things which are not contributing to your goals. Of course, not everyone in your company will know what the 'end' looks like. It is your responsibility as a leader to steer your team towards a bigger and brighter future. If you are consistently clear and communicating your vision and 'end' – whether large or small – this will also help your team understand where you are going, and how they will benefit by contributing to achieve the goals.

For us, we usually assume responsibility for the biggest decisions. There are more than 140 team members in our group, which means over 100 hundred families, whose lives and livelihoods are affected whenever we make a decision, directly or indirectly. That's why we need to always have the end in mind, so that we shoulder our responsibilities to help everyone in our company fulfil their dreams.

When it comes to big decisions, such as acquiring a business or opening new offices, we always adopt end-in-mind thinking. We analyse what it means to our overall vision to achieve this step, and whether it takes us closer to our end goal.

By having the end in mind and realising my responsibility towards my team and clients, I am driven to perform at my best every day. I always remember my leadership has an impact on them.

It's also provides a greater level of clarity to your leadership. For example, not too long ago, I was working on business development with one of my leaders. It was a particularly busy time, and there was a lot going on. She had lost sight of the end goal because she couldn't see how this acquisition would add value to our organisation. So she started to question where all this activity was leading. But she knew I always keep the end in mind, so I explained about the benefits of what we were doing and how that was contributing to our overall goal. Having the end in mind allowed me to communicate this swiftly and clearly. Back on track, she returned to work with renewed energy.

EXAMPLE

This book is a great example of having the end in mind. I took the time and made the effort to write each page, ensuring that the information reflected my views and principles based on my experience. It's taken me away from my business, and it also took up valuable family time, because in order to write I needed to focus, and so I worked on weekends. But I'm not focused on the lost time, because for me, the end in mind for this book was to give back. It's giving back to help people run their own business effectively and add benefit to our leaders to learn from reading this book and develop best practices.

If I can provide value to current and future leaders it will be an amazing outcome for me. This was the end goal when working on this book.

Exercise

The best way to work out the end in mind is to find
a time, by yourself, away from your work environment and
sit alone with a cup of tea or coffee and look at the big
picture. The time away from the office will give you the
breathing space to consider your 'end' and observe what
you are doing to get there with clarity and perspective.

Obstacles will seem smaller and easier to overcome
when you look at the bigger picture. When you have the
end in mind, you will have the ability and power to make
big decisions and keep on moving forward.

Here are some questions to ask yourself:

- Where is your life journey taking you?
- What is the end result you're after?
- What are your current challenges?
- How are they part of the overall plan?
- What small steps can you take today to move
  towards your end results?

- ....
- ....
- ....
- ....
- ....

3. BE NAÏVE

I love this one, because this is about the blind faith that you need in business if you really want to challenge yourself, your beliefs and your foundations. Being naïve is about believing in what's possible, even if it isn't perfectly logical. Being naïve is trusting your gut instinct.

When you are building a business, there are many decisions you will need to face that sound and seem illogical at the time. It may also feel unsettling, which is often the sense of risk or fear manifesting when we know that something exciting is on the horizon. But you must calculate the opportunity cost of not doing something, not just the cost of doing it. If you pass on an opportunity now, how will it affect your business in three to five years from now? Will it leave you behind your competition? Or by pushing the green button, will it help you become an industry leader in three to five years? Will it take you closer to your goal?

Being naïve is about being open to opportunities. A great example is Elon Musk, who is committed to making it possible for humans to move to Mars. He embraces a naïve mindset and believes that if something is important enough, even if your chances of success aren't great, you need to do it anyway. For us, in the middle of 2016, an opportunity presented itself to acquire a major office building with the capacity to fit 30-40 people. At that time, I was based in one of my original offices, but I was missing out on the ability to oversee and lead the whole organisation from a central location.

We were only nine team members at the time. Thinking of moving to a building with the capacity for 30 plus people was a massive capital investment. But once we had a detailed discussion as a team, we realised this decision could be a significant step to achieve our company's vision and goal in the long term. Although there were many unknowns, and it felt like we were stretching ourselves out of our comfort zone, a scary move – we listened to our gut feeling and made the big transition in acquiring this building. We made this our central Head Office for the whole group and set up a great training facility where we hosted our monthly and quarterly training for the whole team.

We also grew our team from nine to 30 people within two years and the move has proven to be significant and the most valued business decision we have ever made. Sometimes, you need to just trust your instinct and embrace the naïve mindset to make great business decisions.

✓ Mentor tip

To foster a naïve mindset you need to calculate the opportunity lost cost for all the opportunities you're looking at and if the opportunity will get you closer to your overall goal. If yes, then you need to take it. Most of the time you'll find fear has no power on paper. Fear multiplies in our head and things can seem bigger than they really are. When feeling fearful, write down all the facts about the matter and you'll find your fear loses its power and you will gain a clarity to make a decision.

Exercise

Calculate the opportunity cost – what would it cost you not to do this? Think through the worst-case scenario in terms of what could result and write it down. Don't leave it in your head. Go through possible solutions to potential challenges. Don't forget to consider the best-case scenario. If you've got a gut feeling, it's likely to succeed.

- What is the worst-case scenario?
- What are possible solutions?
- What is the best-case scenario?
- How can you achieve it?
- ....
- ....
- ....
- ....
- ....

Finally, having a naïve mindset is important because it's your job to lead the mission and create more opportunities for you and your team to grow. Sometimes you must trust your gut instinct.

4. EMPOWER OTHERS

Pure and simple, this is one of the best ways to lead – empowering others. Not only does this give others the ability to lead, but it also enables your business to grow faster, benefitting from shared knowledge and skills – not just relying on yours. It tests ability and highlights the future leaders.

Ambitious people are more engaged, more motivated. This means they perform at the highest level. Letting others take the lead frees you up to focus on the big picture. And, in turn, it empowers *you*. It empowers you to build a business that can run without you one day.

The number one thing I focus on daily is empowering my team to see and do bigger and better things. As a leader your job is to see at an elevated level. You need to build your team to see for themselves and the business. You must believe in people before they believe in themselves – that's an amazing quality in a leader, giving others the belief that they can do it. Taking it a step further, you should give them credit if they succeed, and importantly, take a bigger share of the blame if things do not work out.

Good leaders focus on the strengths of their team members and build on that. They encourage their team to play to their strengths. A good example is our sales superstar, Seema Kaur. Exceptionally talented at closing deals, she was not good with paperwork or marketing, so we gave her more time to focus on her best skill by hiring an administration assistant for her team to look after her administrative and marketing tasks. She focused on her strengths: helping clients in their property journey. Empowering your team members comes in many shapes and forms. It can be in a one-on-one conversation or in a group setting.

A major shift happened for me a few years ago when I attended a leadership session. One of the presenters said that you should treat your team members as if they are volunteers. Sure, they get paid to do their job, but they would get that anywhere else as well. Imagine that they weren't being paid, and that they were with you only because they enjoyed it. This brought a shift in my thinking and my actions in working and treating our team members. I became a much better person to be around and more than ever, I was catching people doing the right things and complimenting them for it.

Success is achieved through enabling others' success. Growth is achieved through enabling others' growth. And everything is about empowering others – full stop!

Exercise

Every single day, think to yourself, 'How can I empower others?' Here are some ways you can do this, some of which we've covered previously in the book:

- *Share the business vision, and values with your team.* We do this at every opportunity, because it helps them focus on the important things and makes the small challenges seem even smaller and entirely surmountable. The more your teams align with the company's vision and values, the better they can perform. If they can see their vision in the company vision, they will be better placed to achieve it.

- *Regular training.* Whether you want to grow your sales numbers or customer experience, the best way to achieve this is to provide your teams with regular training to become better at their jobs. This is especially important once they achieve certain skills.

- *Checking in.* One of the best things you can do is to check in with individuals to see if you can assist them improving in their work. If they provide you with feedback on how they can do better, listen and try to reasonably implement their suggestions for how you can help them achieve more.

- *Group Discussion.* Every quarter we encourage a group discussion on how to improve our current operation. We ask how we can be more effective? How can we tackle individual challenges? How can we provide better value? Once you hold a session like this, you'll find you will have better solutions. When everyone is participating in the solutions you'll notice how empowered they feel to do better.

- *Play the long game.* Business is not a 100 metre sprint. It's a marathon. Just by shifting your mindset to play the long game, you'll find your priorities will shift which will result from your focus only being on today, or the week. You will encourage and empower your team for long-term success.

5. ACT FAST

Action cures fear.

There was an extremely fearful time for me in the early days of the business. The debts were piling up and the business felt like it was going under. I remember being frozen with anxiety. One Tuesday evening I decided to make fifty prospecting calls to connect to my clients.

That immediate action made me feel relaxed and hopeful for the future, as the action itself was fundamental to my role. I continued to make 50 phone calls every evening. It didn't matter where I was, what I had going on, I came back to my desk, made a bitter green tea, and made the calls between 4:30 and 7:00pm. The action was collecting strong pipelines for future client leads. I was making slow progress every day, drilling into the anxiety and fear which began to disappear. This action is now a productive habit that remains with me to this day. I guided my team to create the same habit, which they took on board and now the majority of our sales team gets on the phone every evening to make 50 calls to find more prospective clients and to close more deals.

You've probably heard of the saying 'just do it'? This one's easy to understand. The idea is that whatever your side hustle, main hustle or gig involves, just get it going. Even if you're not ready and want to plan, research and do your due diligence, it's far better to get something happening, so that you have a starting point.

In early 2020 an opportunity was presented to us to acquire one of our major competitors in the Western Suburbs. We researched and realised the huge upside to this acquisition. It would provide a bigger and brighter opportunity for our teams to grow. This acquisition was considered to be one of the best independents in the area. There would be challenges around handling a big operation such as different clientele, team culture, misalignment and, of course, a massive financial commitment. This was when COVID-19 hit and we went into a three-month lockdown. The fear of failure was strong – what if we couldn't handle it? What if we couldn't finance it? The banks were being very strict due to the pandemic. We assembled the leaders together to discuss this and to reach a final decision. We carefully went through our options.

1. How would it help our vision by this acquisition?

2. What would we miss by not taking this opportunity?

In the end, we decided the missed opportunity would be too great if we didn't go ahead with it.

We took action over the next few weeks against the fear of failure. Despite the challenging situation, we went ahead with the acquisition and brought their teams over to ours. We worked hard to merge the two companies. One year on, we're so proud that we followed through on our vision and didn't let fear rule our decisions. The merger has been a roaring success from every angle.

It's easy to make a good decision fast when we have a clear mind and the information we require. It's often not the case in business. Usually, you're dealing with a lot of unknown elements, and you may not feel you're able to make the right choice.

But sometimes, you might need to embrace the idea of failure as a business owner. You will surely make mistakes. This is the opposite to what our culture tells us, 'that failure is bad', and that we should avoid making mistakes or failing the test. Nothing makes failure lose its bad rap so much as doing something, failing at it, and getting over it by trying again or trying something different. Success is never far away.

So how can we cure our fear? Act fast. If we dig a little deeper, it's our emotional state that creates this fear. Our mind tends to live in the past or the future, which is a scary place to be. So, if you act quickly, you can deal with it more quickly. Take some fast action to clarify the future potential and challenges of the opportunity. As mentioned earlier, if you write your fears down on paper, the fear loses its power and you'll have a better picture for how to make an informed decision.

Even more importantly, I'm referring to small decisions made on a daily or weekly basis. When some of these decisions are not made fast enough, they frustrate management and things do not get done. Even when you have bigger decisions, you can take some early steps to find out more. Staying still will cause harm.

Moving fast is exactly the methodology of some of the world's brightest entrepreneurs, including Mark Zuckerberg. In the early days of Facebook, his goal was to move fast and break things, and if you weren't breaking stuff, you weren't moving fast enough.

This approach encourages rapid ideas testing and attracts more feedback quickly, meaning you're more likely to come to solutions sooner. No one understands this better than technology companies, who constantly release prototypes and correct as they go based on feedback. You see this with new apps all the time. As you may have heard, most innovation ideas die in the shower. In business, some of the most powerful ideas die in the meeting, where valuable ideas get shared but because of slow decision-making, they don't survive.

Exercise

When I think about how fearful I was when I thought the business was going down, I remember being frozen by the anxiety. When I started making fifty prospecting calls every day, it cured my fear. The results didn't come to me straightaway, but by acting every day, I was a lot less fearful. Whatever your fear is, you must take action to cure the fear.

If you can bring yourself to act fast, you can snatch success with both hands.

If you are fearful about anything, write about it. A lot has changed for me since I learned that fear has no power on paper. So, whenever I have a doubt or my mind is not coming to a clear decision, I do a brain dump on paper.

1. Write about everything that's on your mind without thinking about it. Clear your mind. Soon, you will find that your mind tends to make things bigger than they are in real life.

2. Once you've cleared your mind, write down the pros and cons of the decision you are about to make. If you are growing your business, you must consider the cons of not making the decision. How will it affect the team and the results of the business?

3. Think about the effect of any decision three to five years from now. How will it shape the future of your organisation?

4. Write down two to three immediate actions you are going to take to find clarity and solve your challenges. By taking these actions you'll find your fears will disappear.

1. ....

2. ....

3. ....

Gather the data you need and decide quickly. You're better off making a mistake than never doing anything. If you aren't sure, test before you do things for real, or roll out a staged approach.

6. TAKE LESS AND GIVE MORE

Hands down, this is a really rewarding philosophy you can adopt for life, and one I personally live by. It's about putting your team's best interests and your clients' best interests first. In today's world where everyone expects more from every relationship or transaction, you can win in a big way if you give the slightly bigger half. It gives great satisfaction if you're looking after your team members and giving them a bigger half of the pie – a philosophy for life. Be kind and give without expecting anything in return.

Taking less and giving more is about making your team winners. This leads to higher performance, which leads to repeat business from clients. It builds trust and helps set you apart.

When we acquired our competitor's agency, this was about giving more to the clients and providing more opportunities to the team. This enabled us to attract two or three times the business we were previously getting.

I live my life by the philosophy that when you give without expecting back the universe will give you many times more in return. I still recall my early days in Salesforce when I was doing really well. I was still helping some of the new guys, showing them how they could be better at their jobs, without expecting anything in return. They were clearly appreciative of the additional assistance and respected me for my efforts. Many years later a number of those guys joined Reliance as Real Estate Professionals and they were aligned with the values and did a fantastic job in bringing the brand to the next level.

I have built my company on staying on the lower end of the stick. Every time I design a remuneration structure or plan growth with one of our team members, we put ourselves in their shoes to see how they will feel empowered. Our rewards are above the industry average – this is a prime example of giving more. And that bit of extra has built loyalty and respect in the team – they want to stay with us as they recognise they're receiving the best pay structure and the best training support, to fulfil their dreams.

Similarly, we train our team to deliver more on client service and on delivering an excellent result every time. Delivering more than a promise helps us to build a pipeline of loyal clients who want to do business with us, as well as refer others to us.

7. TAKE NOTHING PERSONALLY

This is the final piece of the leadership puzzle. And perhaps it's also the hardest. Business can be unfair which is nothing new, and at times you will become disheartened.

You will manage multiple things in your business at the same time and learn that you can't be across everything in the business, as much as you'll want to be. It's inevitable that things will happen outside your control, perhaps in an area where you have not paid enough attention. This means that you could miss noticing things which you might need to address. You will have obstacles and challenges you'll need to handle. While those challenges aren't nice to deal with, you should take the opportunity to learn from every situation and keep moving forward. Let go of the negative energy, and realise that it's not personal.

It's usually not about you. When you take things personally in the office, you take it home with you. It affects your home life and you're not who you need to be. You're not who you need to be for the business and equally, you're not who you need to be for your family. This can also affect your energy and mindset while working on other things. It will affect you. So, you need to learn from it. Try instead, to minimise the feeling of hurt. In that way, you can have good, clean energy to spend on other things.

Letting go of people has been one of the hardest tasks for me – I used to take it personally every time. But eventually, I learned to let go of any negative feelings for the person. I looked at the situation from their perspective – they believed they had found a better opportunity or platform. I would then wish them well. Analyse the situation to see if you can do something better, learn from it and then let them go. There can be many other things in business you can let affect you personally, like losing business to competitors, non-performance of team members, an argument between team members or unreasonable demands of teams or clients. But taking things to heart will only deplete your good energy and positive attitude and have an impact on other areas of your business and personal life.

EXAMPLE

As I mentioned in the introduction, everything felt like it was falling down when things were going badly in the early days of the business.

I knew it would be tough, but I hadn't understood just how tough it would be until I began to take hit after hit – team members leaving one by one. The hardest thing was seeing my top performer, Ravi, leave. He originally followed me when I started the business.

He wasn't making enough money, had a new family to think of and was presented with a better offer. I couldn't expect these people to follow me blindly when things weren't looking good for the future. His leaving felt very personal, and I was disturbed by it. How could he do this? But then I looked at it from his perspective. It took some months to realise that it was not personal. His circumstances were changing and as things were not looking bright with Reliance, he had to secure his and his family's future.

The big shift happened when I didn't take things personally and kept in touch with him as a friend.

I'd outlined earlier how after two years had passed, I approached Ravi to rejoin me and to expand to a second office. His return was an incredible strength to me and my team. It worked so beautifully well for us. We expanded the business to double our numbers and grew our office from one to two and were recognised for the fast growth. The lesson is none of this would have happened if I'd taken things personally and not been willing to look at things from his perspective. I later realised it was a very important test for me, and that out of it I learned resilience and gained valuable skills to build a business from the ground up.

As I discussed earlier, I am a morning person, and a major shift occurred once I began a morning yoga and meditation session each morning. Meditation has been a major game changer. I achieve mind silence for a few precious moments. I experience peace and ease. I also practise meditation in the evening after a hard day at work. I aim to remove any negative feelings about an event or a person. Different things work for different people.

Some of my colleagues feel revived and refreshed after a hard gym session. It doesn't matter what it is, as long as it works, and you find a way to ease your mind to let go and don't take these situations personally.

✓ Mentor tip

It's natural to feel bad when something doesn't go as you expect. And it's natural to feel hurt when someone does something that affects you adversely. But you can't have this attitude as a leader. Learn to let go.

Exercise

Training yourself not to take things personally is a huge asset. Use this short exercise to practise putting yourself in someone else's shoes. Think of two events, past or present, where someone has distressed you. Perhaps they've failed to deliver something promised to you on time, behaved unprofessionally or left you in the lurch so that you've had to do extra to make up for their actions. Perhaps they've gone back on their word or resigned without notice or explanation.

Now, go back over it. Allow any residual negative feelings to wash through you and let them go. Make the conscious decision not to take it personally and ask yourself, 'Can I see this from a different perspective?' What learnings can you take from these events? Take away the fact that the event adversely affected you and come up with reasons why these things could have happened. Experiment with seeing things from another side.

1. ....

....

....

....

....

2. ....

....

....

....

....

Some behaviour may have been unprofessional and unacceptable in a work context and may need addressing with further investigation, feedback or a performance review. However, as a leader, such processes should be undertaken objectively and fairly, without it affecting you personally.

Summary

- Everything is a skill, so you stand a brilliant chance at developing all the business skills you need with great success. One of the key traits of leadership is appreciating your team and encouraging them to be the best version of themselves. We covered seven steps:

  1. *Own your mornings.* Start your day early and start it with a routine that will give you energy and ownership of your day. You'll be amazed at the positive effects.

  2. *Have the end in mind.* You're the captain of the ship, responsible for steering it in the right direction. This means always being clear on the vision and keeping your people aligned and motivated to ensure you move forward.

  3. *Be naïve.* If something is important enough, you should commit to doing it, regardless of the bad odds. You must believe in what's possible, even if it's not completely logical, and follow through. Trust your gut feeling.

  4. *Empower others.* Even if they doubt themselves (especially when they doubt themselves). This gives others the ability to develop leadership skills, and creating leaders is one of the most powerful things you can do as a leader.

  5. *Action cures fear.* This is about making decisions fast and acting on them. This is how you make progress. This is how you grow. And your people need a fearless leader to follow.

  6. *Take less and give more.* This is about putting other people's interests first. It is about making other people winners.

7. *Take nothing personally.* This is perhaps the hardest part of the leadership mindset to master, about recognising that while business can be unfair, it is not about you. You are the one who must step back, try and see things from the other side, and let go of bad feelings that will fester and hinder your progress. A wise leader lets go.

CULTURE IS SIMPLY A SHARED WAY OF DOING SOMETHING WITH PASSION.

BRIAN CHESKY

PRINCIPLE FOUR

CREATE A THRIVING CULTURE

I'm sure you've heard the phrase it takes a village to raise a child. Well, I think you need to build a village to create a thriving business! And then, what about a thriving business? To achieve this, you need to prioritise creating a fantastic environment for your team to come to work in.

If you think about the leading tech giants in the world, they are passionate about providing an excellent working environment, which enhances wellbeing and productivity for their teams. Not only do companies like Google, Facebook and Amazon invest in incredible-looking headquarters that showcase state-of-the-art campus-style designs, but they also recognise the value in making the workplace – where you most likely spend most of the week – an environment that promotes team wellbeing and joy.

After all, where would you rather work? Somewhere unfriendly, dour and lifeless? Or somewhere welcoming, lively and colourful, a place where you find camaraderie and fun every day?

Prioritise having a fantastic environment to work in, where people can become friends with one another, have fun on the job and encourage each other to perform better. That is why I always wanted to create an environment where people feel welcomed, looked after and part of a high-performing team, family, tribe and community.

Studies show that social integration is one of the strongest predictors of longevity. And it turns out that the relationships you have in your life, regardless of whether they are people close to you or simply people you chat with throughout each day, are very important. The idea is that the more happy social interactions you have, the happier you are and the longer you live.

The amount of social integration you can engage in at work – the place where you spend such a vast amount of time – is an important factor in your health and wellbeing.

Some people think that work is a place to be serious, a state to be kept separate from the things you enjoy. But I believe if you have a happy and fun work environment, teams feel great about being there and ultimately production goes up and you are also surrounded by positivity.

So wouldn't it be better if our workplaces embraced a culture of friendship where we are encouraged to interact with our teammates and create lasting relationships? Where we are invited not just to compete with them and other businesses, but also to collaborate?

Of course, all of this is easier said than done. As we know when it comes to anything to do with success in business, it must stem from the top. Setting the tone is very important. I am a big believer in culture being caught, not taught. It's mainly shaped by the leaders. They need to live and breathe the culture. How do they act? Do they work as team? Are they living by the company values? We do not use words like employee or staff – we address our people as 'team' and 'team members'. We are all part of the same vision; one team with one goal.

BUILDING A THRIVING ENVIRONMENT

In our group, we are always working to create an engaging and united team culture which encourages team happiness and better productivity. An environment where people want to spend time achieving their goals. It's where they perform the best and they feel empowered by the other team members. No one is clock-watching, waiting for 5pm to grab their things and go. They feel happy about coming to work and contributing to achieve a shared vision and success.

One of things I'm most proud about our organisation is the connection, friendship and respect for each other. There is genuine bonding among teams. Everyone feels like they are part of a large, growing family and work in small teams to achieve the best outcomes and results. We heavily promote friendship within the workplace, which engages a higher level of relationship within team members and plays a huge part in workplace happiness. We believe in integrating our personal and professional lives to ensure our families are a part of the company's culture. This is evident when we're invited to celebrate our team member's wedding overseas, when we go to our colleague's empty new home on their first night to enjoy the milestone, and even when we visit our co-worker's new baby in the hospital and help them choose a name.

We encourage any possibility to bring the teams together throughout the year with a number of events, such as Culture Day, Family Day, yearly awards and so on. However, most bonding happens at the smaller team's level where they get to work closely with one another on a daily basis. In their teams, they go skiing and hiking together, play team sports on the weekends, and celebrate birthdays and anniversaries.

We have casual Fridays where people wear what they want and generate that Friday feeling of welcoming in the weekend. People speak to one another, listen to one another, are there for one another. By creating a happy workplace, we attract great talent and retain them well. Your team culture will play the biggest role in attracting the right people to serve and delight your customers.

All of this has happened by merging our lives. We truly believe that we wouldn't be able to work like we do without our partners' and families' support, and we ensure we recognise this.

In this chapter, let's dig deeper into how we have created our inclusive family culture. I invite you to make changes to your own business environment, and see your own culture thrive.

OUR TEAM VALUES

Developing your team's core values will give you an excellent base for your thriving culture. Our five team core values are the basis for our hiring process, and even our firing. First of all, you need to define your team values. Once you have that in place, then bring in your team members, who embrace those values. For example, teamwork is a very common value, therefore you hire people who are really good at being part of a team. Once your team members are aligned with your values you can reward positive behaviour based on these values.

But how do you align your action with your vision? The answer lies in identifying the values that tie in with what you want your business to become. Then, every action and behaviour needs to be a match to these values.

In our business, our values aren't simply items to be checked off on a list. They aren't words that we memorise for a sales pitch, or lines that appear on our email signatures or business cards. They truly define the *way* we do business. They inform who we hire, how we behave as a team, and how we behave in our company. These values are our badge of honour. They are what make us different. They are why our clients and our people choose to work with us.

- *Reliance is a family:* We support every member of our team to achieve their personal and professional goals
- *Empowering leadership:* We grow leaders within by cultivating an environment of creative flexibility and trust and providing opportunities to grow

- *Embracing growth:* Constant improvement is a priority. Regular in-house training helps our team develop their business and life skills

- *Respect:* We respect the differences of culture, opinion and performance within our team

- *Fun and celebration:* We make it a priority to celebrate both personal and professional achievements.

One of the most important elements is creating a respectful and caring environment in our business.

We show clearly that we have respect for every member of the team, and it's not dependent on their performance or any other

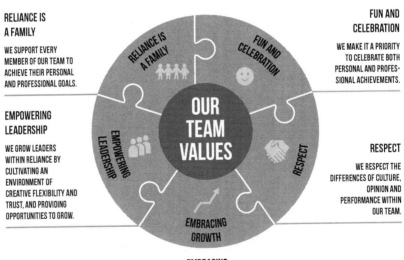

RELIANCE IS
A FAMILY

WE SUPPORT EVERY
MEMBER OF OUR TEAM TO
ACHIEVE THEIR PERSONAL
AND PROFESSIONAL GOALS.

EMPOWERING
LEADERSHIP

WE GROW LEADERS
WITHIN RELIANCE BY
CULTIVATING AN
ENVIRONMENT OF
CREATIVE FLEXIBILITY AND
TRUST, AND PROVIDING
OPPORTUNITIES TO GROW.

FUN AND
CELEBRATION

WE MAKE IT A PRIORITY
TO CELEBRATE BOTH
PERSONAL AND PROFES-
SIONAL ACHIEVEMENTS.

RESPECT

WE RESPECT THE
DIFFERENCES OF CULTURE,
OPINION AND
PERFORMANCE WITHIN
OUR TEAM.

OUR
TEAM
VALUES

RELIANCE IS A FAMILY

FUN AND CELEBRATION

EMPOWERING LEADERSHIP

RESPECT

EMBRACING
GROWTH

CONSTANT IMPROVEMENT IS A
PRIORITY, WITH IN-HOUSE TRAINING
TO HELP TEAM MEMBERS
DEVELOP THEIR PROFESSIONAL
AND PERSONAL SKILLS.

element. Even when an individual might be different to the rest, so long as they are part of the team and doing their job, we treat them with respect and foster everyone's wellbeing. For example, if someone is not a high performer, but they're a good culture builder and team player, they are just as valued and recognised as a part of our team.

This is because we genuinely take care of our people. We support them through the good, bad and ugly times. People need to feel cared for in this uncertain world – they need to know that their company has their back and can offer them security and certainty.

Exercise

How can you create your own set of core values? Think about how you live your life and run your business. What principles do you adhere to? What is important when it comes to dealing with work and dealing with other people? What factors come into play whenever you are making a decision? What are the foundations upon which your business is built?

Write a list of five values that resonate most with you.

Now, delve deeper. Ask yourself *why* these things are important to you. Rank your five values and write about them here:

1 ....

....

2 ....

....

3 ....

....

4 ....

....

5 ....

....

Creating shared values: I remember we were only a group of 45 team members when we created our values. The best and most effective way to create shared team values is to get your team involved in the process. Gather your team into a creative space and explain the main reason why you want them to create these values together. Give them an understanding that this is how teams will work together and how an uplifting and encouraging environment is developed. Give everyone a blank page and have them list how they would want to be treated in the workplace and what is important to them. Each person can fill out their list of up to 10 values or behaviours. You can also provide some examples.

Allow a relaxed atmosphere and enough time to complete the task. (Another good option is to give them a week to complete this on their own time, thereby giving them space to reflect on what they would like to implement). Once you've gathered their sheets, place them into groups where people have listed similar values and behaviours.

You should now have 5-10 values or behaviours to work with. You need to make decisions yourself, or with your core leadership group, as to which top five most align with your vision.

Once you've created your list of shared values in the brainstorming phrase, share them with others in your business – at every level and in every department – to see what *they* think the priorities in your organisation are, and why. Add to the descriptions of different values with input from your team – and from your customers.

Now, this list should have five values everyone agrees upon. Even if you don't have a team yet, still aim to create your core values. They'll be what you believe, and what aligns your team. These are the values to live by each day, in every aspect of business. Promote and celebrate them.

1 ....

....

2 ....

....

3 ....

....

Now, how do we create this environment and values? We do it in three ways:

1. a culture of communication
2. idea sharing
3. fun and celebration.

1. A CULTURE OF COMMUNICATION

Communication is one of the most important components to creating a happy workplace.

You can bring some top experts on creating a thriving culture, but you can never outsource your culture. It starts with you and your leadership team. One of the first major steps you can take is to have a transparent and honest conversation with your team.

It is how you learn about anything that is going on – through talking to people and listening to what they're really telling you, and letting them know they can bring any topic to the table. This is how to build trust.

One of the most important skills you can develop as a leader is to learn to speak last. Give others enough time to share their opinion, ask questions to clarify how they have come to their thought process.

When people feel listened to and their opinion is valued, they are empowered to do their job well. When they are encouraged to speak up and share their opinion, everyone benefits. Our culture is about how the team feels when they come to work. A sense that you can really *talk* to people is the first essential element of a great culture.

> ✓ **Mentor tip**
> In crucial conversations, you don't want to hear the words, but the words between the words as well. You don't want to hear what someone says but understand what they really mean. The attention you give to someone by listening is the best gift you can give.

The better the culture, the easier it is for team members to say what they mean. Often, they'll give us hints. 'I like doing this,' they might say. 'I'm good at this.' They may be asking us to notice what they *don't* like doing so we stop asking it of them. Once you have a clearer understanding about what they want, you can work with them to create a tailored solution. You start to learn about an individual – how to treat them and how to encourage them to perform at their best to make it a win-win situation.

If the culture isn't one of communication, not only are people left wondering why certain things are happening, but bad feelings get buried, to fester and stew, and issues aren't managed. Any talking is done in whispers, and behind the backs of the people who might be able to make a difference. Leaders can sometimes be surprised when people show their discontent by leaving at the first opportunity – they may genuinely not have known that anything was wrong. You should manage issues directly with the relevant team member. Listen to them carefully, what is their concern, and what is the cause of it? I have personally experienced that if you listen to your team member with full attention, more than 50% of the concern is depleted by listening to understand.

In our wider team, our leaders are very well connected with their teams. Teams know if there is an issue or challenge, and they can share freely. When a challenge or problem is being expressed, you not only have an opportunity to resolve it but you can also make a bigger impact by investigating if a similar challenge is also happening elsewhere in the organisation.

For example, one of our office coordinators explained that there was a lack of connectivity with others in similar roles and there were some unorganised tasks she found frustrating. Through a quick survey we found the issue was also experienced with others in similar roles. After a brainstorming session with all involved, we introduced the morning huddle. It's a short, sharp 15-20 minute meeting to enhance clarity around organisation for daily tasks. We get a greater understanding of what is happening throughout the day with every office. Most importantly, all office coordinators share a very good connectivity with each other and learn from each other.

By encouraging a culture of communication, you will enhance your culture immensely.

One of the best ways for us to promote and connect team members is through the six-weekly breakfast initiative. We invite 8-10 team members from different departments/offices – the idea is to have people around the table who wouldn't normally have the opportunity to sit down with each other. It is an opportunity for them to connect, get to know each other, share ideas.

Things to consider:

- share the company vision and purpose at any opportunity you get
- hire and fire people around your team values
- encourage people to have transparent communications.

2. IDEA SHARING

In our business, team members are encouraged to stand up and contribute their ideas. We create opportunities for ideas to flourish.

But how do you do this? One of the best ways is to give your team the opportunity to contribute to solve the challenges and be a part of the success of the business. Let them voice their ideas and give them the satisfaction of seeing what transpires. This is how you create a business that innovates rather than sticks with the way things have always been done.

Let's go back to communication. Tell your team their ideas are welcome. Tell people that the possibility of failure isn't the worst worry, and that their ideas won't be discouraged. Ask them, 'Do you want to try something new to improve?' Tell them you want them to try. Invite them to tell you their new ideas. If the ideas flow, you empower people to run with them.

Then, test their idea. Ask them how they would implement it and break it down into steps. Give them the freedom to experiment and say, 'If it doesn't go according to plan, don't worry. It's okay. We can fix it. Or try again.' Of course, not everyone is full of ideas, and some people prefer to follow others' ideas rather than initiate their own.

As well as ensuring everyone understands our approach to ideas and failure, we also hold more structured and formal brainstorming sessions. Every three to four months, we hold a mastermind session of top performers in our head office.

We encourage them to share ideas to see what can be done, what should be the focus, how we go to the next level, what needs to be implemented.

✓ Mentor tip

If your team is worried about their ideas failing, they'll never try anything new. But when everyone is given the opportunity to shine, everyone sees that they can contribute and that their ideas are given every opportunity to succeed, it promotes responsibility, accountability and progress.

So, how do you incorporate idea sharing into *your* culture?

Exercise

Host an 'ideas session' where your team is invited to attend and brainstorm ideas to create and improve productivity. Offer feedback and encouragement.

Have an open discussion to share current challenges and let teams come up with possible solutions. In the second half of the meeting, you can discuss how to improve the teams' wellbeing and happiness collectively. Alternatively, ask people to submit ideas for their department in an ideas box or through an online survey. Select one idea a month or quarter to implement and announce it to the organisation.

3. FUN AND CELEBRATION

Finally, we get to the enjoyable stuff! Having fun and celebrating the wins are a vital part of creating a thriving culture and we are so serious about this we have turned it into one of our most important team values.

As well as the other values we've discussed, a great culture is one where people find reasons to celebrate. They go out of their way to celebrate, and they celebrate both others and themselves.

In our group, we celebrate professional achievements and big and small. It is fair to say we look for reasons to celebrate.

Of course, when we are nominated for and win awards, there is a massive celebration among the whole team. The Australasian Real Estate Results Awards (ARERA) was a big one in 2018 – the business won Metropolitan Agency of the Year, I won Principal of the Year and our General Manager won Support Star of the Year. We attended the awards ceremony and shouted about it from the rooftops. Since then Reliance has been blessed to be recognised as the fastest growing real estate company in Australia and was awarded a further two times in a row. I won Australia's Principal of the Year for the next two years and was inducted into the Hall of Fame.

In terms of how the business is going, we don't simply look at the big results. Whenever anyone achieves a great success or does their personal best, it's cause for celebration. When someone has a delighted customer, when someone's had their best month, or quarter, when the business achieves a milestone, when the business itself has an anniversary, when new recruits join and when the team achieves their very best – these are all worthy of celebrating.

We celebrate personal achievements, too. We take notice of any occasion deserving of a celebration, big or small, because we believe that celebration always brings people together. On someone's birthday, the company WhatsApp group consists of lots of messages from all the team wishing them a great day. The office then comes together briefly to share cake and give a gift and card. The same happens when someone gets engaged, married or has a baby. It's a celebration of happiness. It makes people feel good and is a great culture builder. Everyone enjoys it and everyone performs better because they feel valued.

Another example is the first day for any new team member. We all know how nerve-wracking day one can be, so we ensure whoever is starting receives a warm welcome from the whole company, with an introductory email or WhatsApp message from the whole team. The office will then hold a brief morning tea to introduce everyone to the recruit. It's the same when someone leaves; we ensure we honour their time with us. We look at their journey with us, what they've contributed, and we wish them well for where they're going next and their future endeavours.

Importantly, each celebration doesn't have to mean big, expensive events or presents. Little things count. It doesn't always take something huge to make someone feel special.

Early in 2019, I introduced my daily gratitude messages. Within the first few hours of the day, I take the time to think about one of my team members and why I am grateful for them within the organisation. I then relay this to them briefly in a morning message to start their day right. It's about celebrating them and their contribution! It is simply taking the time to let them know they've done a great job – small things make a big difference. It means we value their time and effort.

We also introduced a monthly 'Behind the Scenes of Reliance', as well as monthly video/email which is distributed to all team members at the end of each month. This outlines things like new team members, team member milestones, recognitions, upcoming birthdays, anniversaries and any company updates, designed and created in a humorous and light way, with a lot of GIFs and photos!

✓ **Mentor tip**

The upshot is that there's not enough celebration in the workplace. Celebrating makes people feel like winners. It adds positive energy to the atmosphere. Why wouldn't you want this in your business?

EXAMPLE

Here are some of the things we do that inject fun into our environment:

- We always decorate and exchange gifts on holidays. We make a big deal out of different occasions, whether it's Halloween, Valentine's Day, Ramadan, Diwali, Christmas, Mother's Day, Father's Day, Red Nose Day!
- We organise an annual Ladies Night for our female workforce and the partners of our male team members to attend. This has become one of the most anticipated events in the calendar.
- We play pranks and practical jokes on one another on casual Fridays. We have something called 'Scary Fridays' where people tend to hide and jump out at one another, trying to give one another a shock.
- We embrace a 10-50 rule: 10 minutes of goofing off for every 50 minutes of focus and hard work in an hour. We believe

micro breaks make people more productive. It's better for your health to move around often. You can't focus all the time, or you can burn out.

- Every quarter, every office has a team building fun event together. As a team they get to decide what it might be, whether it's bowling and dinner, go-carting, or even a boat trip.
- We have a highly-anticipated annual event/anniversary. The excitement we build is fantastic and goes for months. This is a themed event where everyone makes an extra effort and it's a fun and excellent celebration for the whole team.

It's important to remember that building the culture is due to the people you employ, rather than the objects you place in the office. You can let your team know you prioritise fun, which is great but if you employ fun people the office will naturally become a fun place to work!

Exercise

Let's celebrate! What events, achievements, personal or professional milestones can you think of to celebrate in your own organisation? Take some inspiration from the examples above. You can always find reasons to celebrate if you take the time to look.

List five and start marking small and big occasions on the calendar that you can commemorate in different ways. Give different team members ownership of different celebrations and let them get creative.

1. ....

2. ....

3. ....

4. ....

5. ....

Business can be tense, and it can be tough, but the place where you work doesn't have to feel that way. Yes, we're at work, but we don't have to be serious all the time. A culture of fun creates a culture of happiness. You can enjoy the time you spend in the office. You can look forward to coming to work in the morning.

How can you inject some fun into your workplace culture? Name three to five things you could add to the office, whether daily, weekly or monthly, to make work a more playful place to be. Make this a team activity and open it up to the group – you'll soon have scores of ideas to choose from.

1. ....

2. ....

3. ....

4. ....

5. ....

Summary

- *Your culture is your brand.* It's what attracts people to working in your organisation and keeps them feeling happy there. We spend more time at work than with our loved ones, so it's important to create an environment where people feel welcomed, looked after and part of a family and community.

- *Success leaves clues.* If you look around, you'll find every success-ful company has a great culture. This is the component that provides a platform for people to excel.

- *By prioritising* the essential elements of a great culture and living them, leading by example and showing your team how to adopt them, you can make your workplace environment flourish.

- The first element is creating *a culture of communication.* Learn to listen or even better, learn to speak last. Encourage people to talk and share their opinion, both to you and to one another. Communication is essential for trust. Listen, be honest and don't shy away from the difficult conversations. Be open with your colleagues and they will be open with you.

- The second is idea sharing. This is how businesses innovate! Encourage your team to share ideas and don't discourage failure. When everyone feels like they can contribute without fear of failure stopping them from trying, it enhances the whole culture.

- The third is *fun and celebration*. This isn't just about big parties for remarkable achievements or something to do on the holidays. You can always find something to celebrate, big or small, personal or professional.

- There is not enough happening at work, period. Encourage your team to celebrate each other's achievements at every opportunity. Try to bring more fun at work. One of the best things in life is fun.

VISION WITHOUT EXECUTION IS DAYDREAMING.

BILL GATES

PRINCIPLE FIVE

FOCUS ON EXECUTION

Execution simply means taking your plan from paper to execute it to make it a reality. It means getting things done. It means having the right systems in place to get done what it is that your business does, whether that's processes for the actual work, your perfect onboarding program, or ensuring your customer experience is at exceptional level. At the end of the day, you can have your vision, strategy, culture and leadership – all the things we've covered – but things still need to get done.

If you can't effectively execute, it's going to be difficult for you to start achieving your goals, let alone the dreams and vision you set out at the beginning of your business journey. If you don't execute, you will ultimately end up more frustrated, because you'll be directing an inefficient use of resources and it will take a lot longer to achieve your vision.

This is where the rubber meets the road. Dreaming is the easy part, in a way. But making things happen is the hard part. It's where you must get into the nitty gritty of how things in your business can be made to work. How can it be done? Who should do it? Whose responsibility is it? This requires a unique skill set for acting decisively and seeing tasks through to fruition. It can be daunting. But be brave!

Not long ago, we had a big idea. We wanted to host a real estate auction event where we would sell several properties on the one night.

Auction Blitz was born! This had never been done in the western suburbs to this scale and we needed to do it right. There were a lot of challenges behind the scenes that needed to be ironed out, as a first timer. Even the team was a little unsure about it! It's often the way when you're trying something new that hasn't been put to the market before.

We first ran an open forum, sharing discussions with the teams who were involved in the process. The whole team was on the same page, seeing the huge benefits it would bring to them, and to our clients. We, as a team, had a detailed discussion about the process from start to finish. We shared some challenges and brain-stormed the possible solutions and suggestions to overcome these challenges.

We delegated various tasks to the teams involved in the process and gave ownership to one of our upcoming leaders. We also agreed to check the progress of the event three to four times in between and booked those meetings in advance. Our idea turned into a goal, then a plan, following the right steps and getting the right people involved. We made it happen.

The Auction Blitz was a brilliant success. We put nine properties under the hammer and sold eight of them on the night where everyone involved executed their jobs well. It was a beautiful night where we created great results and a positive impact for our clients, together as a team.

As you'd expect, through this event, we also learnt a lot, particularly with training our in-house auctioneers. Until that date, we had only hired external auctioneers. We selected five team members to go through a rigorous training process to become auctioneers. We hired an outside auctioning firm to train our selected team members, as these exceptional, selected individuals are the specialists in auctioning our properties. They gained an extra level of confidence and expertise under their belts and as a result, we not only made the auction a great success, but gained expertise in in-house auctioneering.

So how can you execute effectively in your business? First, you need to identify all the elements and everything that needs to be done, and then work out the process required to bring your goal to fruition. If it's bigger than one person, you'll need to delegate accordingly. Identify the people who you believe can run the show and instil that belief in them. Review the action plan and make sure all the different elements are implemented properly. Award responsibility to different people for various parts of the process. When it all comes together, that's the dream.

In this chapter, I'll share with you my four steps, the key stages required to execute effectively:

1. systems and processes
2. delegation and ownership
3. effective meetings
4. implementation and reporting.

✓ Mentor tip

It's important to note that if you are only focused on execution, it can contribute to your business becoming an unpleasant place to work. People won't be driven to achieve anything special. That's why it's important to balance execution with culture and leadership.

---

1. SYSTEMS AND PROCESSES

Systems and processes are defined ways of getting stuff done. Creating workflow, efficiencies and capabilities for dealing with change. Ideally, you want to put procedures in place for any task that needs to be done more than once. By working out the best way to do things and making sure they are done in the same way consistently, you'll avoid unnecessary issues.

So, how can you figure out *your* systems and processes? Through observation, the use of technology and alignment to your business strategy you will improve performance, results, engagement, and ultimately create greater success for the business. What you want to do is have a deep-dive into your business. Break it up into five or seven key areas or phases, and then their sub-areas.

For example, there are several stages in the buying experience, the period from a call to a lead, or from a prospect to an appraisal. In these phases, we 'market', we do letterbox drops, we prospect. When we go from 'appraisal' to 'list', there is another phase with other defined procedures. We send out a letter every three months. We give clients a call. Then, at Christmas, we send out a gift and card. We need to have anywhere from 8-12 formal communications. These can include text messages, phone calls, letters and emails. Then, when we reach the list to sell stage, that's a whole different process.

That can be broken down into two or three parts as well. 'Sold to 'settled' is another process. Afterwards, how you treat those clients is important.

So, you can see that one business will have many segments. You will be aware of all of them but perhaps haven't thought about them as opportunities to introduce systems and processes, which will help you increase your efficiency and potentially increase your profits.

After you have your phases, make a list of the frequent tasks that are performed within each. Each of those tasks needs a simple step-by-step set of instructions.

EXAMPLE

Let me share with you something that cropped up for us in the early days. Back then, we always struggled to have the keys ready for clients when they came into the office, finishing settlement after buying a new house.

Sometimes, we couldn't even find them! The office coordinator would bear the brunt of this when owners were, understandably, annoyed that they couldn't pick up the keys to their property.

This was a failure of our settlement process. We were great at listing and selling properties, but from sold to settlement, we were crap! Our customers consistently rated us 4.8 or 4.9 stars out of 5 for our services when they were surveyed upon signing but when we were rated at the time of settlement, it was 3.8, 3.5, even as low as 3. Not so great! Our system was terrible from sold to settlement.

Understandably, the sales team's focus was serving new sellers and buyers in the property transaction. Older news was practically forgotten. Sometimes the clients would have to call, as they were unaware of the next steps.

It was the kick we needed to review our execution. So, one of our office coordinators was given the responsibility and she set up a checklist designed to itemise the process. She would establish a week in advance which properties would be settling and which owners would be coming in, and not only organise keys to be ready for them, but also a settlement gift and congratulate them on their big step.

Today, keys and settlement gifts are always ready when someone comes for them. We built a process where our clients are very happy with the sold-to-settlement process.

✓ Mentor tip

It's a good idea to make your process and procedure list easily accessible online so that everyone can refer to it and see it. In more advanced cases, you could also create a video recording of someone going through a process.

It's advisable to go through a testing phase, where the step-by-step instructions are trialled with members of the team to see if they can achieve results or whether more work is required. Once things have been tested, they can be rolled out across the different departments.

Once everything's been shared, it's important to revisit your procedures regularly to review them. You should be constantly improving and refining them.

Having a system with detailed processes means anyone can take on a task. It achieves consistent results. It prevents mistakes. And it means there's an accountable record of how things should be done.

Exercise

Identify the three to five major phases that need to be broken down in your business, for example, your accounting system, your sales system, your support system, your inventory system, back office or front office. Then, identify the tasks in your different departments that get done more than once. Are there systems and processes in place to manage these tasks? If not, what are the end-to-end processes involved? Once you've made notes, you can give someone the responsibility of getting all the details from process owners and creating policies, procedures and flowcharts which the current team can refer to and new team members can learn from.

1. ....

2. ....

3. ....

4. ....

5. ....

Every single part of the client experience is important – the aftercare as well as the main event. The things that go on behind the scenes that support the work you do in front of the clients are critical to smooth operations and good client experiences.

2. DELEGATION AND OWNERSHIP

As a leader, the core of your business is learning how to do business, doing it and then teaching it. It's hard to do everything yourself, so it's time to delegate along the way.

Delegation is fantastic because it empowers others. It frees up your time for the work you must do as the head of the business, and in turn, your people become more skilled and fulfiled over time. It sets the tone, too and you will act as a good example for other leaders in the team.

But delegation can be difficult, and managers struggle with this all the time. It's hard to let go of something you've built and have control of, and most times you will feel that you can do this better, but it's essential for progress. If you're bogged down doing all the essential tasks, how do you have time to grow the business?

Furthermore, it's unreasonable to expect that you're an ace at every single aspect of your business. It's completely unfeasible. You may be awesome at prospecting, but terrible at paperwork. So, delegating will work wonders to keep you working at your strengths and bring exceptional results in the long run.

Over the years there have been two areas in our business which have brought tremendous success in delegating and giving ownership to other team members.

The first area – in the early days of my business journey, I was doing most things myself, including the day-to-day accounting.

Accounting is not what I enjoyed. It was crucial to find a qualified accountant who could take care of the accounts side of the
business. It was also time to give others responsibilities, rather
than having everything start with me.

We found a qualified accountant who was totally aligned with our
team values. Since he came on board, he has taken full responsibility of the day-to-day accounts and all the short- to medium-term
planning on the accounting side of the business. Now my responsibility takes one and a half to two hours a month to go through
the numbers with him. It has not only given me more time, but
now I'm confident that things are being handled by someone who
is qualified and an expert in this field.

The second area – I had a strong skill in selling and customer
service, but I wasn't so strong in managing rentals, and neither
was my team. We employed someone to take ownership in our
rental area. This was someone who had extensive rental experience, and who had managed and grown rental teams in his
previous twelve years in real estate. As our new head of the
rental department, he was responsible for hiring and supporting
our rental team, and impartially providing an excellent service
to our landlords. He could go ahead and change things, add to
things, restructure various roles. He had complete autonomy.
I was there to empower him and support him, but he was driving
this area.

Since he came on board to lead the rental department, we have
increased our rental business by 200% and growing. Within twelve

months, our client satisfaction has increased, and more referrals have started flowing into the department.

This is an issue of scale. How much can you achieve if everything must start with you? And how much autonomy can you offer others if you must be the one to try something first?

As your business grows, you won't be able to learn, do and teach everything. Empowering others to take things forward means that you can do a better job as captain of the ship.

Execution is about finding the right people to take things forward and get things done. You might be the owner of your organisation, but how can you give others ownership?

As we covered in our fourth principle, you should consider what it's going to cost you not to delegate?

How can you get into the habit of delegating? The key is figuring out which things you do that are essential – which things *must* be done by only you – and which things can be achieved by someone else. In a time-poor environment, this is essential for efficiency.

It might be helpful to keep a journal of everything you do across a week, and a month, and list out *all* the various tasks. Which of these tasks can only you do? Which of these tasks can someone else do? Which of these tasks can someone else be trained to do?

Exercise

Review your journal and consider all the tasks you do on a daily, weekly and monthly basis.

Write a list of five things which you could delegate, either by handing them over to someone else whom you are aware already has the skills to do them or by upskilling someone so they are trained to perform that task.

Hand over these tasks. Help them to create a process for people to follow and train them to do it as you have been doing it. Oversee the training, then hand it over completely.

1. ....

2. ....

3. ....

4. ....

5. ....

✓ Mentor tip

Do the work to delegate the tasks that you do not need to be doing yourself and perform this exercise at regular intervals. It will empower your team and will create growth opportunities for individuals and the organisation together.

3. EFFECTIVE AND REGULAR STRUCTURED MEETINGS

Meetings, with good rhythm, are the heartbeat of the organisation. They must happen on a regular basis. They are also the key to communication and decision-making. As your organisation grows, you need to hold regular, structured meetings to provide the good oxygen flow required in the growth stage. Not communicating with key people can slow down the growth, and this can impact the whole organisation.

It is essential that the meetings run efficiently. No one likes it when someone from accounts waffles on or goes off-topic at 9am on a Monday morning. Show your team you respect their time by keeping your meetings short, snappy, effective and valuable.

We have daily, weekly, monthly, quarterly and meetings set up in advance in the team's calendar. And we make sure they run like clockwork.

Daily meeting

Departments hold a quick 'standing', huddle meeting, 10-12 minutes short, quickly running through the focus of the day, what the priorities are and any challenges team members are facing.

The office coordinator of each office also attends a 15-20 minute, daily Zoom call. This meeting is to see if each location is equipped for the day to serve the clients who are going to walk through the door, regardless of whether they're in the diary for a pre-booked appointment or they walk in out of the blue.

Both these meetings are scheduled each day to keep them account-able for daily tasks, giving them a sense of purpose. A bonus is that by dealing with issues upfront, it saves the whole team writing unnecessary emails to each other with updates, because they discuss anything in advance.

Weekly meeting

As we are a sales-driven business, we have our weekly sales, rental and performance meeting at every office. In these meetings, we discuss the achievements and challenges of the previous week and what we are looking forward to in the next week. The meetings are all about results and customer service, and how we can improve.

Again, this meeting helps keep our teams to stay accountable and on the right track with properties that may have slipped off the radar or deals that may have been waylaid but are back on the agenda.

Monthly meeting

This is an executive meeting where leaders from every office gather with other executives as well as the support team. We discuss the results, opportunities and challenges facing the offices and the group overall. We revisit our yearly and quarterly targets to reinforce our vision and goals for the year. From those targets, we make strategic decisions.

By having the monthly meetings, we could find a solution to almost anything on the spot because each department was there and could hear the challenges others faced directly.

> ✓ **Mentor tip**
> Leadership meetings in person with multiple departments also help create a good rapport between the leaders and support team. The teams feel empowered to approach each other to have their matters heard and solved.

Quarterly meeting

We have all the performers go through the quarterly plan and thoroughly assess what support they need to achieve the targets for the next quarter. This meeting gives us real insight into our clients and what challenges we are facing. It highlights how we can improve our approach to these challenges. Most importantly, we look at our yearly goals and see how we are tracking, identifying which areas we need to improve.

Annual meetings

We hold two main meetings once during the year, designed to target our company culture and our company strategy. The whole team gets together, and we make it fun and relaxing, so that we can enjoy each other's company, and for everyone to feel part of the growth of the business. Both bring us a lot of excellent ideas to work with. We'll select a few low-hanging fruits or immediate fixes that we can implement straightaway, and then make a list of things to work on in three months, and long term across the year, as you'll read more about below.

Annual culture meeting

At this meeting, everyone is invited to have their say, and give feedback on what is working well or what can be improved. They're usually half a day and we come together to play games with a bit of education. One of our activities is to take fifteen minutes for everyone to provide feedback about three to five things they like and admire about the company, and three to five things they think we can improve on. This gives us a list of genuine improvements to work on over the next year. It's a good opportunity for everyone in the company to get together, and provide feedback on how we can improve our culture and performance.

Annual planning and strategy meeting

This meeting is longer than our culture meeting and typically one and a half days, attended by the key leadership team and representatives from each department. In 2020, we headed to the RACV Torquay Resort. In the first half we had a fun team building exercise before enjoying a nice dinner together. We then spent the next day planning and creating strategies to see what we could achieve, as well as focusing on areas for improvement. We ran a range of exercises. We did our SWOT analysis (Strengths, Weaknesses, Opportunities, Threats). It was interesting to hear everyone's contributions. We always attract brilliant ideas. Typically, we'll come up with five to seven quick fixes, then three to five things to focus on for the next 12 months, and a further one to three things for the next three to five years. This gives us an excellent list of items to work on, which contributes massively to our culture of progress, performance and growth.

An efficient meeting comes down to excellent planning to ensure it runs smoothly and offers ways to measure, amend and improve each item as it is introduced for discussion. If you don't have efficient meetings, confusion sets in and your team will become frustrated with the waste of time. To maximise everyone's time, effort and output when it comes to meetings, here are some tips you can use in your business:

- Provide a set agenda

- Set your meetings up for the same time and place to keep them consistent and regular

- Consider forty-five minutes duration, covering all topics and agenda, encouraging the team to move fast and put their points across efficiently. The less time people are given on agenda items, the more quickly they will get to the point of the discussion

- Play background music before the start of the meeting

- Provide ten minutes at the start of the meeting to discuss key learnings for the week

- Start with good news (personal or professional)

- Report on numbers every week

- Come prepared with KPIs and weekly statistics

- Provide items to action

- What is the focus of the week / preview? (open discussion)

- General business – one or two items

- Finish with a great quote or positive statement.

Consider a shorter duration, covering all topics and agenda items. Encourage the team to put their points across efficiently. The less time people are given on agenda items, the more quickly they will get to the point of the discussion and find a resolution. Finishing on time is so important. Meetings are there to save time, not waste time. Usually, meetings run over because someone has a private agenda. In that scenario, see if they can discuss the matter later, offline.

Effectively run meetings help you complete all projects on time and hold everyone accountable to organisational priorities and goals.

4. IMPLEMENTATION AND REPORTING

Most of us overestimate what we can achieve in one year and underestimate what we can achieve in five.

Implementing anything, from a new business venture or office to a new project or process, can feel overwhelming so the best way forward is to take a staged approach. This helps ensure that everything gets done in a realistic timeframe.

We tend to focus on challenges in quarters, or we call it the 90-day race, to see what we can achieve in this time, with our focus firmly upon our goals. We set a priority for each quarter and break that area down into everything that needs to happen successfully to get that project off the ground. This includes planning, considering change management, policies and procedures, project management – everything that goes into achieving a goal.

Once you've put systems into place, delegating tasks, implementing processes or awarding ownership – how do you know if they're all working?

Reporting means you can see whether what you're doing is heading in the right direction towards achieving goals and garnering results. It is the answer to the question you should be constantly asking of your business: how is it *actually* going? Reporting gives you the opportunity to correct things if they're not going as planned and make the right changes accordingly.

But I'm not just talking about measuring results, or even better, progress. Often, what is measured increases. But what is reported can lead to exponential growth. This is because it's about seeing what's being done and asking: Can it be done better? It's a feedback loop from reporting to revision and round again.

EXAMPLE

The implementation involved when opening any new office is a big one for us. When we did it for the first time, we were very green. We had no idea what to expect, and so learnt everything on the job for the first time. Everything was new and things were challenging. We ran three weeks behind schedule, and we were working ridiculous hours trying to pull everything together, because we were also running the business at the same time.

So, going forward, we broke each step into a series of tasks requiring actions managed by the person or team responsible for the step. Then, every action was broken down into a simple step-by-step process. There are stages for implementation which we can address in a timely fashion, with the right roles assigned to different people. We made a 16-step process of opening a new office, which can be easily measured and reported. It worked, and now we can roll out the same implementation for every new office we open, refining as we go.

✓ Mentor tip

Implementation is about breaking things down to build something up. It's also about constant review and improvement. Successful execution requires a focus on effective implementation.

Reporting means taking things a step further and seeing how you can implement things better. Done well, it is a constant opportunity for informed learning about what is working well and what can be improved further.

Exercise

When we report on performance, these are the typical questions to ask:

1. How did we go with various tasks this month or quarter? How do we think we've done performance-wise?
2. What was good about it? What wasn't working?

3. What can we improve next time?

1. ....

2. ....

3. ....

By regular reporting and the right implementation, you can achieve your business goals a lot faster.

This becomes a plan to be executed – and then we ask the same questions on an ongoing basis.

How can you ensure success with reporting? Accountability is important here. There needs to be a person responsible for various reports and for reviewing how things are going and assessing the scope for improvement in discussion with others.

Combining all four steps means you will be a master of execution in your business.

Summary

- If you don't execute well, it'll be much harder to achieve the success you dream of. It's harder to achieve your goals and move forward in the long term.

- Execution is important for keeping your business alive. Of course, everything you do – making a plan, getting people together, working things out – costs money and time, but with the proper execution, you will direct and make the best use of your resources.

- Let's recap the steps:

  - To achieve successful execution, you'll need systems and processes. These are defined ways of getting things done that help you achieve consistent results, prevent mistakes, resolve challenges so you can achieve the desired results.

  - Delegation is next. This involves teaching others to undertake any of your tasks that can be better performed by someone else. This simultaneously empowers them and frees you to focus on other important parts of the business.

  - Regular and structured meetings are there to achieve the best results. Holding effective meetings enables clear communication with key people in the business. Held regularly and with a clear agenda in place, meetings allow challenges to be faced and solved swiftly.

- Implementation and reporting. Taking a staged approach ensures that processes are in place to achieve project goals and things get done in a realistic timeframe. Reporting means a constant feedback loop leading to plans and revisions and results.

- While vision, people, culture and leadership are all integral to success, execution is equally key. Remember, things need to get done!

MARKETING IS THE ACT OF SHARING WHAT YOU ARE PASSIONATE ABOUT.

MICHAEL HYATT

PRINCIPLE SIX

MARKETING YOUR MESSAGE

I want you to ask yourself a big question: What business are you really in?

It may seem silly. I mean, surely you know what business you're in, right? Let's take McDonald's as an example. The fast-food chain is one of the world's most successful franchise businesses, but there was a time when they were going broke and trying everything to get back on the right path. One bright mind asked, 'What business are we really in?' And the answer was that McDonald's was actually in the business of real estate. It was more about acquiring the most valuable real estate sites with more exposure upon which to build their restaurants – not only selling hamburgers – that allowed a successful business to grow into an empire.

Now, turn your attention to your business. It can actually be difficult to see what business you are really in, as it may not be related to what you're selling.

My first business was serving my clients to deliver the best possible results and outcomes for their property or real estate. But that was before we grew to the next level. Now what business are we in? We ask this question as an organisation. The answer is big and bold – we aim to serve our clients to reach the best possible outcome for their property. But when we went deep into it, we understood that we are in business to find new recruits, train them really well and nurture them for future opportunities to grow with our organisation. Ultimately, enabling our teams to fulfil their dreams. Plus, we want them to help our *clients* to fulfil their property dreams. Now for any decision we make, small or large, we keep this purpose in mind.

Consider asking yourself, 'what is your core business?' or 'what business are you in?' This will form the foundation of your core message, identify your target audience and direct your marketing.

The following three points will help you to find and retain both perspective buyer (your external clients) and your team (your internal client):

1. who is your ideal client and target market?

2. what is your core message?

3. marketing your core message.

Once you have discovered the purpose for your external and internal clients, the next step is to establish your ideal client and define your target market. When it comes to your customers, start by noting down who is buying most frequently from you. Where are they from – the local area, online or somewhere else?

Answering this question provides you with deep insight. When you can recognise the most effective ways to reach your potential clients, you can place more focus on your targets. You can then choose how to spend your marketing money.

But the core message itself? How do you deliver it? Who do you deliver it to? This is about getting your name and your unique selling points out to your ideal audience. The better you know who your audience is, the more effectively you deliver your message. If you do a good job in marketing your message to your target audience, then your audience or market will know you and the services you are offering before they need you, and will approach you freely when they do.

1. WHO IS YOUR IDEAL CLIENT AND TARGET MARKET?

How do you achieve success when it comes to delivering your message? How do you know who to speak to? You need much more than a scatter-gun approach which targets everyone and anyone, but only finds a genuine customer by happy accident. To avoid wasting time, you want to aim to strike up relationships with those who need what you're offering, not those who really don't, making them the wrong target. The way you do this is by defining your target market exactly, so you know precisely who to attract, and sell to.

For example, take the owner of a good quality Chinese restaurant in our area. He said to me that most of his diners come from one area of our suburb, so he focused his marketing activity in that area to attract people from that part of town. Most of his deliveries go out to that area as well. He worked out that most of these people have already paid their home mortgages and were quite relaxed about their lifestyle. He understood that many of them had a high net worth, which is how they could afford to pay for his great service, quality and authentic Chinese food which came with a higher price tag. By knowing his ideal client, he knew where to target his marketing. He was aware they were looking for more in terms of quality food and service than they would get from a cheaper, local restaurant, who were busy targeting their customers based on budget. He knew that you couldn't appeal to everybody – but you could appeal to your ideal consumer and get to know them well.

✓ Mentor tip

Do not try to appeal or sell to just anybody and everybody. Have your ideal client profile in mind; understand why they have come to you, and then provide more reasons for them to do business with you.

Our market comprises homeowners thinking of selling their home or investment property. They might wish to sell for a variety of reasons, including retirement, upgrading/downgrading their lifestyle or personal circumstances. Our market is also split by geography in order to achieve a more focused marketing plan. So, we have our target market, but what about our ideal client?

We undertook four days of intense workshop on brand strategy to discover who our ideal clients were. We found that our clients were mostly upgraders, lifestyle seekers and investors. These clients formed our top 80% of the business we attracted. We became clear on our ideal client and then went on to focus all our marketing efforts on these client types.

For our internal client (our team) we know our ideal candidates are driven, energetic, progressive individuals who are looking to excel at their profession in real estate.

To attract more of our ideal team members, we have painted an exact picture of who we are looking for. We target them through specific marketing, and also promote our company culture heavily and highlight our individual team members success by sharing videos, testimonials and reviews.

Once you know your target market, you can generate more customers in the same area. And you can do more marketing to the same customers, as frequency builds trust and you will make it easy for your client to do business with you.

EXAMPLE

Consider one of our top performers, Taney Jain, who has been successful helping over 200 families move every year. It only took him three years since starting his real estate career, which is a phenomenal result.

Taney is very successful because he knows exactly who his ideal clients are – and exactly what message he wants to deliver. He has a defined database of future clients, which is categorised into investors, upgraders and downgraders. They're also classed as hot, warm or cold and he sends out his marketing specifically based on these categories.

Most small businesses do not take time to define their market and their ideal clients. You can simply measure on a daily or weekly basis who is buying from you. In the beginning of this research, as long as you know 50-60% of your consumer demography, you will be able to focus your marketing efforts to attract more clients. But the more you want to grow, the more you need to focus on identifying your ideal clients.

Defining your target market further means that you can draw out clear responsibilities for your team. Each team member can be given an area to focus on. And the better you know your audience, the more you are perceived as an expert. Knowing your market, ultimately, leads to more effective marketing.

So, how can you work out who your target market is? Consider different demographics, such as location (whether on a local, national or global scale), profession, longevity, personality, age, gender, marital status and income. Paint a picture, as detailed as you can, and describe the people you want to receive your message and work with you.

EXERCISE

Here are some questions to consider while creating a profile of your ideal client:

- Where are they from / where do they live?
- What do they do for work?
- How old are they?
- Are they male or female?
- Are they married, single or in a de facto relationship?
- Do they have a family or are they single?
- How much do they earn?
- Where can you find them?
- What do they watch, listen to, and read?
- What activities do they enjoy?
- Where do they shop?
- What other products and services are they interested in other than yours?
- What problems do they face?
- How can you help them?

....

....

....

....

....

....

....

Through this exercise you will get to know your ideal
client better. Over time you'll refine this image to gain
a very clear picture of your ideal client. Once you know
who they are, you can focus most of your marketing to
attract your ideal client.

2. WHAT IS YOUR CORE MESSAGE?

Why should people choose you? It will be hard for them to choose
you if you don't have a strong core message. This is how you
relate to your audience, showing them that you have expertise
and experience and can offer them a better solution and service.
It gives them a way to talk about you to others, with strong, articulate points. If you do it right, it will create some raving fans for
your business who will continue to buy and, most importantly,
will keep referring you to other potential clients.

It is also how people will assess you before they even approach
you. When they meet you, they will ask themselves – does this
business have the best solution and is it best equipped? Does it
have the right vision and purpose? Are they consistent, are they
delivering on their promises, are they walking their talk?

I think one of the biggest jobs in marketing and presentation is to
make it easy for your clients to choose you. While they will know

about you and what you're offering, they will know about your competitors' offering as well, so when it's time to decide, they will compare you with others. If you and your competition are offering quite similar things, it will come down to price. Who is the cheaper out of two or three options?

Therefore, you need to come up with a really strong message and a real point of difference (POD) to make it easy for the client to choose you. You could also call it your unique selling proposition (USP).

✓ Mentor tip

Taking the time to establish your POD is important in the beginning of your business journey, when you struggle to compete with some of the bigger names. You want to give your target market something memorable which will cut through the noise of your competitors.

What is the Reliance Group's POD and core message? 'One team one goal to maximise the sales price/return on your property, while providing you an exceptional experience.' This means we act as one unified team with one goal, to maximise the outcome/return of your property/real estate, while providing you with exceptional client service/experience.

In accordance with our values, we put our clients first as a priority, constantly innovating, displaying passion for excellence, engaging in transparent communication. Our clients rely on us to achieve the best outcome for their property and we work together as one team to help them to fulfil their property dreams. Our core message informs what we do and the way we think collectively as a team to achieve the best possible outcome for our clients.

Every time we market our results online, or through letterbox drops, on a social media campaign, or in our presentations, we make sure our core message is loud. During any presentation we give, we make sure we deliver our core message at least three to five times, to really ensure our clients remember what we're about – it's our unique selling point.

While all our competition is working in small teams and competing against each other, we are united as one team, one goal. Our ideal client wins in a massive way when they work with us to receiving the benefit of the entire sales team members at their service and a collective approach to maximise the result for clients.

Similar to the message to our clients, we have a core message for our current and future team members: 'We, at Reliance, provide the best platform for our team, with the best training, and an encouraging and uplifting environment and an opportunity to grow'.

This is the very reason we became employer of choice for high-performing agents in real estate. We have potential recruits approach us every week to join the business, thanks to our strong core message. It's become a fabulous recruiting tool and we make sure we deliver our promise via the following three steps:

1. Onboarding process: our company is well known for its excellent onboarding. We provide 4-6 weeks of onboarding training

for all new recruits to give them the tools and education for a long-term successful career.

2. Ongoing training: At Reliance, we consider ourselves a training and development organisation which leads our teams to becoming the best professionals.

3. Opportunity to grow: one of the main reasons our ideal recruits wish to join us is due to the growth opportunities we provide. We focus on growing our teams, which in turn enables the company to grow.

Since we worked on our purpose, *enabling people to fulfil their dreams*, it is now a part of our language and our consistent message across social and digital marketing, as well as part of our presentation to all current and potential clients, and recruits.

So, how can you create your own compelling message?

This goes back to a lot of the work you've done so far. You know your purpose, have honed in on your values and have established your vision. What do you want people to know? What are you good at? What makes you unique? What is everyone else doing and how are you different?

Think about things that will resonate with your target market. Our results improved exponentially when we pinned down a clear message.

What can you do to make your target market feel more comfortable? Why should they choose you? Tell them about it!

Exercise

Write down the top three things you want your target market to know about you. If a client were talking to a stranger about you, what three things would you want them to say?

1. ....

2. ....

3. ....

If you had to sum it all up in one simple sentence, what would your core message be?

....

....

....

This could be a good start to your key message. Consider getting your team involved in creating your core message.

3. MARKETING YOUR CORE MESSAGE

Now you know who you want to talk to, and you know exactly what you want to say. But how do you go about it? Well, there's actually no blanket approach. What will work for one business will not necessarily work for another, so it's necessary to discover, through research and perhaps some trial and error, what works best for you. The good news is that once you work it out, you can focus on that and hopefully yield excellent results.

Getting your message out there involves two main groups of marketing activities: paid and unpaid.

Paid marketing is anything you invest money in and pay for. It covers digital, including web development and SEO, print, radio and television advertising, flyers, brochures, campaigns – anything you pay to produce.

Evaluate which paid advertising channels are worth your investment. What is your budget? Can you calculate your return on investment based on an estimated conversion rate? What can you measure? Be conscious of every dollar you spend. We are always asked to sponsor events, at quite a high cost, but often there is no real return on these investments so we stop spending our marketing money on big sponsorship, especially the ones we cannot ensure the return of our investment. Spending your energy and marketing to be the best in the business is much more valuable than putting your name on someone else's endeavour.

Unpaid marketing is a little broader. It includes being recognised, from awards, participating in community events, attending local business groups, receiving favourable media coverage, social media activity, customer reviews, testimonials, word of mouth and much more.

In our group, we get our name out there in a variety of ways. But really, our most valuable marketing efforts are in the unpaid space.

From the signature with which we sign off our emails, to being shortlisted for awards, appearing in the newspaper, being active on social media, being covered by digital or print media for good work and participating in local groups – we strongly believe the time investment is well worth it to be active in unpaid marketing space. Receiving third party endorsement for excellent work is many times more valuable than paying for advertising.

In our early days, we attracted a lot of unpaid marketing by entering awards programs. For the first couple of years, there were no wins and no recognition. But time teaches you to be patient and we kept at it doing the right things to get ourselves to our required level. In 2014 we were so happy when, for the first time, we were named as a finalist in our council's business awards. It fostered great excitement in the team. The council also advertised the finalists on their website and in local print media too, so people started taking some notice of us.

✓ Mentor Tip

I highly recommend business owners enter in awards for their category of business. It is not only to provide recognition among your ideal clients but will also create a positive energy for your team.

When we receive recognition, we ensure we celebrate it. And when we win an award, we are given the opportunity to step up and accept it in front of a crowd of people. We add the award logo on our website, and we attach it to our email signature so customers can see we are finalists, and we share it on social media.

It is an indirect marketing tool that stays in the presence of our audience, one that says we are performing, we are growing, we are achieving industry and nation-wide recognition for the work we are doing. Nominations and awards are a sign of achievement; each one is a badge of honor – so we wear it. This comes at the cost of hard work and your willingness to do more for your team and clients.

EXAMPLE

In 2016, we won our first award – named in the top 100 fastest growing companies of Australia. This gave us huge exposure. We promoted it in our videos, in our one-on-one presentations to our clients, on our email signatures, in local newspapers, on our website – anywhere and everywhere we could.

Adding to our credibility among our clients, we were again finalists in our council's business awards. We displayed the awards' logos everywhere in our marketing materials.

In 2017 we were featured as the eighth fastest growing company in the *Australian Financial Review*. It was the news of the century for us! We were recognised in a few magazines nationally as well as locally. We promoted our win via all the sources we could. At the same time, we won the award in the Medium Business category in the Wyndham business awards. It was just amazing to have these two awards. In any given week, as a group, we give

50-70 one-on-one presentations. Our team's confidence went to the next level. While that was a direct effect, leveraging these accolades and presenting them to the market meant there was a huge indirect impact as well.

All of this is important because it builds credibility in your industry, and it creates opportunities for your team and business to grow. And importantly, your potential clients are watching you and ultimately will make a decision whether to buy from you or not. Every time they see or hear your name associated with good work they get closer to doing business with you.

List two to three award categories you can apply for in the next year. Make sure you read the criteria in advance. In the beginning, if you struggle to fill out the nomination form you can hire an external professional to write about you and your services.

But don't put all your eggs in one basket. Consider various methods that may help you achieve your marketing aims and look at the pros and cons. Below we look at two ways that have worked well for our business over the years.

Networking groups

Consider attending local community groups or professional groups to stay in touch with local businesses and keep the referrals coming in. Specifically, in the beginning I was a part of various networking groups such as Business Network International, Wyndham City Business Group, Australia India Business Council among others. If you join groups like these, with the right interaction, you can direct business, and importantly, you are building your business name among other people of influence.

I remember first joining Business Network International (BNI), which is a group of professionals who refer business leads to each other. We used to attend a meeting Thursday morning at 7:30am to pass on referrals and take turns to give a short presentation about each of our businesses. It worked well to get our name out among other professionals who could refer their clients to our business and vice versa.

If you look around in your industry, you will find several groups who directly complement your business and who can keep you up to date with latest trends. It's important to keep in mind that these groups will only work if *you* make them work.

Testimonial, review and word of mouth/referrals

Once you deliver an excellent experience to your clients, testimonials, reviews and word of mouth will do wonders for your business. In today's digital age, consumers heavily rely on these reviews before they make their final decision whether to purchase from you. You need to find ways for your happy clients to give you reviews online and leave written or video testimonials for you to promote to your audience.

Whatever ways you use to market your business and whatever channels you employ to deliver your message, there needs to be rationale behind your choices. What will a newsletter sent out to people listed in an email database achieve for you? How? And why? Be very particular where you inject your energy – and your marketing spend. Don't just follow what other people are doing, even if they're in the same industry and appear to be doing well, as there might be other factors at play. Instead, focus on what you have figured out will work for you, and continuously review the work you are doing in this department to make sure you are consistently, creatively and effectively delivering the message you intend to impart to your target market.

Exercise

Identify the key paid and unpaid marketing methods you can harness to deliver your message to your target market. Write down the different ways you could approach the market, and the reason these channels will work for you.

Paid

1. ....

2. ....

3. ....

Unpaid

1. ....

2. ....

3. ....

You can always start small by deciding to enter in only one or two awards now. For paid marketing, be very selective with your marketing methods. There are ways to market your business which will cost you enormously with little benefit. Calculate your rate on return for your money spent.

....

....

....

....

....

Summary

- It's important to ask yourself what business you're really in. What do you want to achieve and why? Who are you doing this for? When it comes to marketing, you need to be clear on what you want to say and to whom. Why should your customers choose you?

- Your first step is to identify your target market. Consider exactly who you need to deliver your message to – who is your ideal client?

- Find out about them and come up with an ideal client profile that you can use to ensure that your marketing efforts are put to the best use.

- What is your core message? Next, articulate the message you want your target market to receive. What do you want people to know? Why should people choose you? What will attract them to working with you over your competitors? How can you present this in a simple and clear way that will reach people?

- Finally, market that message and get it out to your ideal clients. This can be done through both paid and unpaid marketing channels. Enter awards for recognition of the business and share your achievements on social media, digital or print and encourage your happy clients to leave testimonials.

STRENGTH AND GROWTH COME
ONLY THROUGH CONTINUOUS EFFORT
AND STRUGGLE.

NAPOLEON HILL

PRINCIPLE SEVEN

LET'S GROW

Welcome to our last principle – growth! So far, the elements we've covered – establishing your vision, taking care of your people, being a true leader, creating a thriving culture, focusing on execution and marketing your message – are so important and create excellent groundwork for any business to grow well. As I outlined in the introduction; this guidance is not solely for business owners who are looking to grow at a rapid pace. These are tried and tested touchstones for those starting out and building from the ground up, to those more established seeking to flourish long into the future, enjoying a great relationship with their team and their clients. That, to me, equals a happy life.

But these principles are not the whole story when it comes to rapid growth; there is a seventh piece to the puzzle. It's the growth mindset, and it affects four key aspects in terms of expansion:

1. people
2. strategy

3. cash

4. execution.

To begin, let me share our own growth and some of the key highlights and opportunities for our team growth.

The group was pronounced 2018's tenth fastest growing company in Australia by *Australian Financial Review*, the fastest growing real estate agency in Australia three years running and won ARERAs a number of times. I took home Principal of the Year and have since spoken at a number of conferences.

I have been recognised in the Hall of Fame awards for winning Principle of the Year three times in a row. I have been interviewed by the media and nominated for Businessperson of the Year at the council business awards. Our offices have meanwhile been recognised as top performing in their area and have won a number of real estate industry awards and recognised for growth and customer service.

Today, we operate from 10 offices with over 140 team members, still growing with high expectations and always looking to provide bigger and brighter opportunities for our team. In any market we open, our aim is to become one of the top three real estate agencies in that market within the first 12-18 months. While the real estate market experienced a pandemic, and many businesses did not survive, we came out of the pandemic a lot stronger as a team and as a business. We believe that our business will continue to grow, even in a down market.

> ✓ **Mentor tip**
> The first four years of our business were the hardest, working 12 hours a day, 6 days a week, without seeing any real progress. You will doubt yourself, as I did in those years, but success is in nurturing the patience and discipline to keep going when you're not seeing any real progress.

I compare building a business to growing a Chinese bamboo tree. When you grow a bamboo tree, you fertilise and water it on an almost daily basis, but you don't see it grow. It won't emerge out of the ground for a very long time. In the first year, it won't even come out of the ground. In the second year, it won't come out of the ground either! You need serious patience and discipline to keep going at this stage when you are seeing no progress. It is the same thing for your business.

In its third and fourth years, it doesn't break the ground but you are still fertilising and watering it. Working hard, you're taking on all the stress of the daily struggle, with nothing to show for it. But keep the faith. Trust the process and you will rise above it. For in its fifth year, the bamboo tree will break through the ground, and grow 90 feet tall within a few weeks and keep growing at a rapid speed.

If you ask the bamboo tree whether it has grown 90 feet tall in five years or five weeks, the answer is five years. During those years, if you stop believing in yourself and stop doing the required work every single day, it will die in the ground.

The same thing applies to business. If you have the end in mind, you need to keep doing the basics to accomplish something meaningful in business.

THE CHINESE BAMBOO TREE

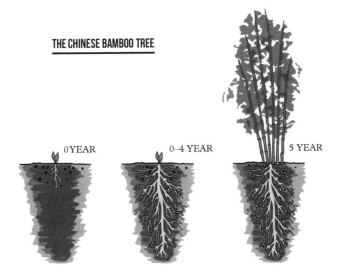

0 YEAR   0–4 YEAR   5 YEAR

Like the bamboo tree, at the beginning of your business journey, if you're working hard and have all the points covered that I've mentioned throughout this book, your business *will* grow. But it will grow its roots first. This is the right kind of growth. You do not want to grow without strong roots or a strong foundation. A lot of businesses have opened three to five branches quickly without growing roots, but that sort of growth is nothing to be proud of – the business won't last very long without a strong foundation.

So, if you are in business and it's not growing at the speed you want, but you're doing all the work, stick with it. Remember, you are trying to grow a bamboo tree. This will take time, but it will grow quickly when its roots are stronger, lasting long into the future.

COMMON MISTAKES

It's only natural that you are going to make mistakes as you start building your business.

The focus is 'natural' because failing is just as important as succeeding, and they'll pop up from time to time organically in the ways you do or don't do things. Frustrating as they can be, mistakes and failures are a necessary part of growing. So, my advice is to embrace the failures, learn from them, so that you can avoid them from happening again. Here is an insight into our experiences and common mistakes I see business owners often make when they want to grow.

EXPANDING WITHOUT THE RIGHT SYSTEMS AND PROCESSES

You've probably worked out that I'm all for growth. But what I see many times over is growth without a game plan. Given that I've spent much of this book emphasising the importance of instilling the right systems and procedures, it makes sense to get this right before expanding.

This plays out commonly with every business if they wish to open multiple branches in different locations but haven't got the right systems and procedures in place, if their main business. It is surely a recipe for disaster.

They think that the next location might make things better for them, and that any issues they have delivering the best service or maximising the potential in one location will dissolve in the next.

They don't realise that if you have a headache in one location, it will quickly become a migraine if you open two more without curing it. Instead, you need to address the challenges of your first location and improve your systems and processes for your customers and your team before expanding.

EXAMPLE

I learnt through a case study that a big business like Masters was introduced to compete with Bunnings and other big stores in the building materials space. The management had a plan to open multiple mega stores around Australia. Once they opened the first one, management quickly realised a big gap in their customer engagement operation including systems and procedures, instead of working to close those gaps on their first location, they turned a blind eye and went on to open 63 mega stores around the country. As most of us know, they failed on an incredible scale and had to close all their stores.

GROWING OUTSIDE YOUR VISION

It's easy to get sucked into the many different types of growth in the business world, but you need to stay on your path. Ask yourself tough questions – how will this new growth bring in more business than you're currently handling? And how will this new growth *really* help your team? How will it help to achieve your business vision?

You need a valid reason for growth beyond just getting bigger for the sake of it, with obvious and tangible benefits. For example,

I've seen companies open a new site simply to gain one up on their competition. They see their competition grow by opening a new restaurant or office, and they think they should follow suit. In other words, they've acted outside their vision based on what other people are doing. What is right for one business is probably not right for another.

There are so many distractions in today's world, especially when you're trying to grow a business. You will see the opportunities in many different ways. But not all opportunities are good; in fact you need to choose one which will get you closer to your company's goal and vision. I also have fallen into the trap. For six months, we diverted from our core business and while running the growth of Reliance Real Estate, went into the investments of land development projects, which took a lot of my energy and focus away from the core business and our vision.

When we realised we were going off track, we quickly wound the projects up and brought our full attention to our core business. I learned my lesson by personal experience. Now I am very careful where I put my energy and attention. When we make any decision, we ask ourselves – is this taking us closer to our vision? If the answer is no or even partially no, we stay away from that opportunity.

I have often been asked the question – why do we only grow in the outer western suburbs? It's a good question. Simply put, every location we add to our network is to benefit the previous locations, and its existing team has to feel empowered by the growth. It's also another location for our clients to connect with us.

LET'S GROW. SO LET'S GO

A lot of wisdom is available on any topic in today's digital age. As Tony Robbins says, 'Success leaves clues'. I have learned from many people who have become successful by either reading about them, listening to them and watching or participating in seminars. Now that I've shared with you some aspects of our own growth, and you have read about some of the mistakes we have made, we're ready to move onto the ways we have grown so much so quickly using our seventh principle.

I want to show you how you can make your business grow in line with your vision, illustrated by the ways we have achieved growth ourselves. As you read on, you'll see that growth is down to four key aspects:

1. people
2. strategy
3. cash
4. execution.

1. PEOPLE

Your people are the first and most important part of the equation. Most business leaders fail to understand the importance of finding and nurturing the right people. In my opinion, this has been undervalued in business. Many leaders start hiring anybody who comes their way, but you must watch out for people who do not share your business values.

In the very early days when I had a business partner, his aim was simply to hire people who would work for minimum money or in some cases, for no money, just to gain experience. That created an enormous amount of work for us around teaching them what we do, even down to basic tasks like how to answer the phone or upload a property online. I learned that in that time you will end up paying anyway – either you pay with your time or you pay with money. These people were not motivated to work, they would most likely gain experience and move on to a better paid job. In my opinion, it is so much better to reward your team with money than too much of your time.

Your business plan is as good as your people, so make sure you have the right people joining you in your business from the start. You need both growth-orientated and process or task-driven people in your business. In the beginning, you might not be able to afford the experienced people who come with the higher price tag, and I recommend having a combination of new energetic team members and experienced ones. The new ones can get training and learn from the more experienced team members. Your experienced team members can also manage more responsibilities, so you can also devote your time to your strengths, where it's most needed.

For many years, I was in two roles within the business – a high-performing agent and part-time CEO. But since 2019 I made the shift to becoming a full-time CEO, leading the group and empowering our team. This saw a significant shift in positive energy and performance of the whole team. It meant my immediate team and I were more focused on training, as well as providing the best platform for every team member to perform at their peak or best.

It's important to revisit your position to analyse where you are most effective in the business. One of the most important roles you will play as a leader is putting the right people in the right seats. Most specifically, the right leaders in leadership roles, people who can lead by example and also handle the pressure of leading a team.

✓ Mentor tip

You need leaders to grow. An individual who is allied with the company culture is one who is ready to walk the hard path with you. Someone who has proven themselves in their current role and is ready to take on bigger responsibilities.

EXAMPLE

When we are looking for our own leaders to take on bigger and brighter roles, we have referred to our five-point checklist:

1. *High Performer* – A true leader must lead by example. This individual has to be performing at exceptional levels in the correct role, achieving their goals and be a role model for others. Only someone who is achieving their goals can teach others how to fulfil theirs.

2. *Focused leaders*– A focused leader with the right energy and drive is important. These attributes, along with a strong skill set, enable focused leaders to lead their teams towards success.

3. *Team players* – We only achieve great things in sport or business with a great team of people. It's hardly ever done alone. Specifically for a leader, it is most important to be a team player to build a winning culture and a healthy environment for everyone to perform in.

4. *Integrity* – This value is what you'll discover at the top level in leadership in any sport or business. It is how they fulfil their promises and whether they do what they say they are going to do. When you lead a team of people but you lack integrity, you will find it hard for the team to follow you.

5. *Natural leaders* – Leaders care less about themselves than the people they are leading. They have much responsibility, are ambitious, and they're willing to do more for their team by supporting them and leading them to a brighter future.

I know these qualities are a lot to ask for in today's business world, but in our business, we don't settle for anything less. If you can find these leaders, hold on to them because they will lift your business to the next level. By having the right people on your side, the sky is not even a limit.

2. STRATEGY

Growing a business is like a game. The more you play, the better you get at it. You aim to do it a little better every time.

If you learn from others like we did over the course of our years in business, you can minimise mistakes along the way. You'll also do things a lot faster and better than if you are muddling along solo.

While we discuss our wins and strengths, it's only obvious we talk about our failures as well. In 2017, we planned to open two offices together. We didn't do much research in the area. We thought we had a winning formula and we skipped some basic steps of research and strategy. Within six months we started experiencing a tough time in this location. Once we had actually undertaken research, we found the area was one of Melbourne's top five suburbs where people didn't sell for a long time – the average was seven years, compared to almost double in this area. But it was too late for us. We had to make a decision. Should we continue in this area, or close the branch and cut further losses? Finally we made the choice to close and we moved our team to other office locations.

We've learnt a lot since we opened our first office, and now that we're planning our eleventh, we're a lot more strategic about growth.

As the saying goes, success is a lousy teacher. We learnt a lot more from our one failure than from our many successes. We really noted the 17 lessons we learnt from our office closure. And as a result, we are wiser and always undertake research when expanding to any new location.

One aspect of our strategy involves intense research into any new market we expand into. We need to know the population, the number of dwellings, the number of investment properties, the number of sales per annum, the competitors and the average selling time of the homeowners and much more.

If our figures stack up, we know we're going to achieve our vision in that area. We've also become better over the years at putting a plan together. As I previously outlined, our overall strategy and goal is always to become the top three agencies in the area in which we're opening a new office. Everything we do is done with this goal top of mind.

For your own growth, it is crucial to put in the research, numbers and hard work in your strategy so that you have a starting point and an end point. I highly recommend undertaking a high level of detail, because it's the only way to really map and plan your success. Once you know exactly what you want to achieve from your growth or expansion, then it's easy to put a strategy together. You can work backward from your three-to-five-year plan, to put in place the right strategy for the first, second and third year, to achieve your goals and vision.

3. CASH

Cash is the lifeblood of any business, and there needs to be enough, especially in the beginning, to cover invoices and associated business expenses.

A business needs to generate enough cash, continuously, to meet all the demands of immediate and future requirements. It can be a stressful and frightening place to fall if you find yourself in the trap of low cash flow and you can't meet the business's day-to-day needs. You may have to borrow money, pay interest, or liquidate investments to generate the required cash. I have been there, and I do not wish anyone to experience this stressful situation. It affects performance at work and the stress spills over to your personal life.

Your ideal position is to generate enough cash to pay all bills and wages on time. Each industry faces its own challenges in improving cash flow. Areas to improve include ensuring you have a good accounts team with great receivable and payable processes. This will certainly improve cash flow.

Many people think cash is the biggest hurdle when growing a business, and certainly this can be true. I have studied a lot of growing businesses and from our own experience as well, it's clear that cash is an important part of the equation, but it may not be the most important aspect. I still believe people come well before cash. If you have the right people, they will contribute to make the business successful, despite being low in cash. By our own experience, in two of our top performing locations, we only contributed minimum cash. We were successful because the leaders were extremely dedicated and had amazing skills and high performing teams.

Cash can be a limiting factor, preventing business from opening. Without a loan or funding, most people don't have enough personal savings to launch their new business. Some very talented and passionate people can get stuck when starting a business and find they lack the cash on hand for start up costs such as leasing, equipment, furniture, recruitment, licenses, advertisement etc.

Cash is obviously a requirement. Don't assume that there is only one route to getting cash. There is a saying, 'where there is a will, there is a way'. You will have to be strong. There are many ways to generate or organise cash. Some strategies for this are listed below.

Organically generated cash

This is the best way to grow your business, especially in the beginning. Our aim was to generate enough income so that we could support our growth. We used capital to set up any new office with all the inventory and team members it needed, and a continuous cash flow to cover ongoing costs. Before we opened our eighth office, the business was totally debt free. We did not have any loans. We had been funding our growth with our own generated cash flow. It was when we acquired other businesses, like in Sunbury and the acquisition of the major competitive agency in Point Cook, that we went to the bank to get finance.

Bank loans

Banks are the major source of funding. Generally, the bank lends about 60% of the total purchase price. If you're looking at a new set-up, then bank loans are harder to obtain as they can't see the cash flow. But this is still the most reasonable interest rate and terms you can get for a business venture.

Business loans are normally unsecured. This can make them expensive and hard to get approved. But they are still great for startups and growing a business.

Borrowing against equity

This is often the easiest way to obtain a cheaper interest rate. Loans against equity are secured against your assets, so banks are more comfortable lending at a low rate. If you have a home or an investment property in which you have built equity over the years, you can easily borrow against it. This is the most common way to finance your first venture. Over time, you build equity in your business through which to fund your business growth.

Private lenders

There are several private firms who are willing to enter into business loans. Generally, they are expensive. They normally want to see your business plan and income projections. There are some private lenders who offer business loans from $20,000 to $500,000, but they come with high interest rates – anywhere from 8-15% depending on the terms. I would suggest staying away from these types of loan as much as you can. This kind of debt can add up quickly and become an ongoing headache.

Equity/investor partners

You can also raise funds by having equity partners. In this case, you must prepare your business plan to show the potential of your business. An investor partner can come on board as a shareholder in your business. They can also be a silent partner offering capital investment or an investor with a fixed interest rate, or you can get them as your investor partners in the business.

We are now becoming wiser in planning our cash flow for our new ventures.

Now when we are looking to open an office in a new area, we know there will be the major cost of a lease, normally up to three months in advance. Then you need a marketing budget for up to six months and, most importantly, six months' finance for all the fixed and variable costs of the business. You will do a lot better in your day-to-day operation if you have the finance sorted in advance.

Sounds a lot, right? But if you count these costs up front and source your finance wisely, you can simply perform better in your business.

✓ Mentor tip

It's good practice to have six months' worth of operating expenses set aside for your new venture or have an arrangement with the bank or another source to arrange funds should you need them.

4. EXECUTION

This is where the rubber hits the road because execution is the real name of the game. Speed is the new currency! In today's economy, it's not the big who beat the small; it's the fast who beat the slow. Having speed on your side gives you a huge advantage when you're a small business, because you're often nimbler than larger organisations who have numerous stakeholders, and who need more approvals and a longer lead time to turn concepts into reality. How soon and how well you can execute a good idea and action your business plan really will decide your business future.

We've learnt a lot of lessons on this – some good and others not so good. As the group has grown, one of the biggest lessons has been that a good plan on paper is only good if you execute it effectively. In the beginning, we used to verbally give each other responsibilities to work on when it came to our plans, but we've since improved and now know exactly what individuals are doing and who has the responsibility to perform which tasks. It provides great clarity to each team member and holds them accountable.

A well-executed plan has a major impact on the success of a new venture. Take, for example, opening a new office. There are different stages for implementation that need addressing in a timely fashion, and each step is broken down into a series of tasks requiring actions managed by the person or team responsible for the step. You can set up the right timing to check the steps are taken; for us it was a week and when it came close to opening we were holding meetings every third day for quick updates and to ensure we were working well on the execution. It's also very important that the right roles are assigned to the right people.

We keep refining our procedures after every execution to make further improvements. In the beginning we did not have any listed plans, but we learnt from our experiences. Our team came up with the first basic plan and we kept on improving it. Constant improvement is integral to successful execution. To focus on improvement when it comes to implementing systems and processes across the board, we have a focus plan that breaks the year down into quarterly themes.

We review systems, procedures and processes in line with these quarterly themes and identify where we can improve. We run training sessions that complement the themes. And we implement changes.

EXAMPLE

Our major acquisition could be the best example of excellent execution. We were given the opportunity to take over one of our major competitors, a very busy agency in Point Cook. The agency is a bustling office located at a very busy and prominent shopping centre. I was involved in negotiating the whole deal. Once we finalised the deal and secured finance for it, it was our business support team who were assigned tasks broken down into five different roles. We met every third day to check if there was any hurdle in executing this plan on time. With an excellent team, we were together able to execute the acquisition on time and merge another high-performing team with Team Reliance. The better we execute as a team, the more fun and easier new projects will become. Your team will feel empowered and fulfiled, and everyone is the winner in a win-win situation.

Summary

- *You are exactly where you deserve to be, not where you desire to be.* This statement doesn't exactly fill you with confidence, does it? I used to dislike this statement very much, but it didn't change the reality. We all think we should be at a higher level than the one we're at today, but the honest truth you know deep down in your heart is that your commitment and genuine efforts have put you exactly where you're supposed to be. If you want more and better results, you must put in more effort and have a genuine commitment towards your aims or goals in life.

- When it comes to growing a business these four fundamentals have worked exceptionally well over the years. We are still learning and improving in each of these four categories as we grow.

- *The first is people.* You need the right people to grow. So, to win people with leadership qualities, empower your team and invite them to step up to grow as individuals and take things forward.

- *The second is strategy.* You need to have a plan. If you know exactly what you're aiming for and keep the end in mind, you can keep on track, stay focused and put your plans into action.

- *The third is cash.* You need to have funding. There are various ways to source this, but whichever you choose, make sure to do your research up front and be aware of your potential costs.

- *The final element is execution.* Plans need to be executed well for growth to go smoothly. Break everything down into steps, assign the right people responsibility for their implementation, and constantly improve your systems and processes.

- We could not have imagined ten years ago that we would reach this level. But we were putting in the hard work, even when we couldn't see the progress. Like the bamboo tree, the business has grown strong roots with unshakeable foundations. Rapid growth is possible for us, and it will be possible for you, too, if you treat your business the same way.

NO MATTER WHAT LIFE THROWS AT
YOU — WHAT YOU MAKE OUT OF IT
IS UP TO YOU.

SADHGURU

CONCLUSION

In my life, I've experienced highs and lows just like anybody else. Some have made a big impact. To finish my book for you, I'd like to revisit two of the major impacts in my business life.

The first is from the introduction, August 25, 2004.

If you recall, I was 21 and set to leave my village, Kurukshetra. I was preparing to leave home for something I hoped would be bigger and better, and my friend, Pardeep, presented me with the Parker pen. He'd said to me, 'I know you will write a unique story with it – make sure it's a positive and inspiring one.'

At the time, I couldn't imagine what my future had in store for me, but I knew that I wanted it full of passion and fulfilment. Now, you are holding that unique story I promised to my friend seventeen years ago. How far I've come!

Through this book, I want to pass this wish on to you and every reader. We are all writing our own stories, so make sure you are living a story which is inspiring to those surrounding you and to the wider world. We need more leaders who are willing to do and stand for the right things. As humans, all of us are craving love and happiness. I strongly believe that together we can create a positive and happy world for ourselves and, importantly, for the next generation.

The second moment I'd like to revisit is February 23, 2013.

If you recall, I'd slept on the floor in my office. I'd had a massive argument with my business partner and in that moment, I felt I had no place in the world.

So, armed with nothing but a crushing feeling of defeat, I ended up sleeping on the floor with my suit on.

But look what waited around the corner! The most incredible experiences of my life – both personal and professional. The moral of this event is that we do not have the ability to judge the future based on current events. Do not give up. Most of the time, your darkest days are the ones holding a key to your brightest days. And on those brightest days, you'll feel so on top of the world, the darker days will simply smudge into the horizon.

Who would have thought that following both these events would be the level of success I could only dream about? Certainly, at those moments, not me! But following the principles that I've outlined, and inspired by my own upbringing and personal philosophies, I have reached a level of fulfilment in personal and professional life that fills me with joy.

Throughout this book, we have visited the different elements that have made my life and business what they are today. They are foundations you can rely on to build a business that thrives too:

- **Vision** – What do you want to achieve? Where do you want your business to go? Having a vision is integral to getting there. In this chapter, we looked at how to define your vision as well as how to align everything your business does with this vision.

- **People** – Being in business is all about people. Your team members are the ones who help you succeed, who look after your clients and represent your business. It's so important to look after them in return. This chapter addressed how to find the right people for your business, how to train them properly and how to take care of them.

- **Leadership** – Being a strong leader is about much more than simply controlling what your company does. This chapter covered what you need to know about having a leadership mindset, from having the end in mind, being naïve and empowering others to acting fast, taking less while giving more, and taking nothing personally. This principle addresses what it takes to be a true leader and how to empower your people.

- **Culture** – The environment you nurture in your business makes all the difference to attracting and keeping the people who will make your every endeavour flourish. In this chapter, we looked at how to create a culture of communication, idea sharing, celebration and fun!

- **Execution** – Actioning your ideas and putting processes into practice is just as important as coming up with a vision and overall strategy. Without proper execution, only the limited can be achieved. This chapter addressed how you can design efficient systems and processes, delegate departmental tasks, hold effective meetings, implement and manage processes, and award responsibility and ownership to others.

- **Marketing** – Your core message is about what you want to communicate to your ideal audience through your branding and marketing efforts. This chapter took you through identifying your target market, articulating your core message and marketing that message through the variety of channels available to you.

- **Growth** – Let's grow! Finally, this is about the mindset that matters when you're looking to achieve real growth. This chapter covered how you can take things to the next level through your people and strategy, with the support of well-sourced cash and careful execution.

Over the years, I've learnt so much – good and bad – using these principles as my guiding light. With hindsight I can see now that every negative is really a positive lesson in disguise hiding around the corner. It pops up in my mind from time to time and I am so appreciative of what it teaches me!

For example, I clearly remember one of my mentors telling me that whatever we do, we do with either love or fear. I couldn't really understand this at the time, but I do now.

I can see I acted out of fear when I opened one of our offices in what seemed like a lightning fast, three-month process. We skipped the right research and preparation. We acted out of jealousy, wanting to look bigger and better than our competition. But the process wasn't fun, and it didn't feel good once we achieved what we set out to achieve because of how we went about it. We had a goal for the sake of having a goal, but there was no satisfaction.

Don't take it personally when the path of someone connected with you and your aims diverges from your own. Always try to learn from their successes, or failures, as you do from your own. And focus on creating your own legacy and writing your own story.

When I talked about my name appearing on the front page of the newspaper in 2017 I was chasing recognition. Benefits like publicity and receiving rewards can be thrilling for a moment, but they are not providing you true fulfilment or satisfaction.

Since then, I've made sure to learn my lessons and to act out of love. As a follower of several different spiritual personalities, I resonate strongly with Sadhguru and the Dalai Lama, who said all we as humans want is to be loved and happy – that's it. Most of the time, happiness only comes from the inside – we shouldn't seek it outside in materialistic things.

The same goes for business. Of course, there is a real thrill in growing a company and getting new people on board to be part of your team.

But I think happiness can also represent the growth in the happiness of your team, creating raving fans as your customers and really enjoying your work – not just happiness in growing your company size and revenue.

Of course, you can follow my principles, learn the lessons and dream of taking your business to the next level. But without simply being a good human, you won't feel fulfiled on your journey.

All along my journey, this key theme – to be a good human and care for others – has underpinned everything. No matter what has happened on my path, whatever dream I have been chasing or whatever vision I have wanted to see come to fruition, I always remember to put others before myself. I could not have survived some of the lowest periods in my career without the support of the people around me.

I know now my real purpose in life and business is to enable people to fulfil their dreams. I want to have a positive impact. I strive to provide an excellent opportunity for my team to learn and grow. In turn, this helps me to build a long-running, successful business that looks after its people and helps me become the best person I can possibly be. This kind of growth equals happiness to me.

It's important to remember that you don't have to be a big business to be the happiest place. I know some businesses with five or fewer people are the happiest places and produce excellent results for their clients. The team feels well looked after and well-connected to the vision of the company – they have a great culture. It's a game you can choose to play – how big or small you want to be.

Have a vision and align every aspect of your business with your values. Invite people into your team who will help everyone flourish.

Create a culture that attracts good people to join and creates an environment which encourages them to stay. Lead them well and be a true captain of your ship. Focus on execution as well as a good strategy.

Deliver your compelling message to the ones who matter. If you get stuck, remember to pull yourself out of the drama and look at the bigger picture – always keep the end in mind.

But remember that the journey must be fulfiling. Life is short. Success is a journey, not a destination. Yes, you've heard these clichés a million times, but that's because they're true! So, make sure you enjoy the journey of getting to your dreams. Every now and then, stop in stillness and ask yourself: Is this really something I want to do or achieve in life? You want to climb the right mountain. After all your efforts, you don't want to feel that you have climbed the wrong one. And in the end, it doesn't really matter what you've 'achieved' – you gain real satisfaction from the people around you. Have you helped them or made use of them? When people value you because you've had a positive impact on them – your life is fulfiling and worth living.

Whatever business you are in, be kind. Work colleagues are more than cogs in a machine – they are people with their own hopes and aspirations.

Competitors are not your enemies – they are people striving to achieve something in the same field as you. You have more common ground than reasons to oppose one another. More things to learn from one another than to fight over. Make sure you empower the people you surround yourself with.

Above all else, your business is you. The more you do, the more you will attract. It's the founder, or leader, who needs to become more, so try to open up more. Become better at everything you do, whether it's marketing, selling, anything – it's in your ability. Always strive to be better because your business will never outgrow you. It's up to you how much you want to grow yourself – that's what will have a direct impact on your business.

And believe in yourself. Enjoy the journey. Be kind. Be a good human. And good fortune will follow.

ACKNOWLEDGEMENTS

I sincerely wish to thank my mothers. Yes, I am lucky enough to have two of them. My mother, who has given me all the major lessons in life – I still have not found a teacher better than her. And my mother-in-law, who has supported me unconditionally through good times and the not so good times.

The third woman I wish to thank is my beautiful wife, Ramandeep Kuar, who has loved me on my most difficult days and supported me every day. Even when I work almost twelve hours a day, six days at a time, she is a superwoman, juggling so many things so that I can stay focused.

My lost friend, the late Pardeep Rana, is the best human being I have ever come across – thanks for teaching me the most valuable lessons in life. Thank you to my brothers, Mukesh Kumar and Parveen Panjeta, who have always stood by me, no matter what the situation is. My family always supports and encourages me to do my best. For both my boys, Arshaan and Armaan, I hope you will learn some good lessons from this book, someday.

Most of all thank you to my Reliance family, each and every member. You guys are the main reason I do what I do every day and I am grateful beyond words to lead such a talented and dedicated group of people.

A huge thank you to my clients for trusting me over the years to handle some of the most valuable transactions of their lives.

To all my teachers and mentors, family, friends and well-wishers, thank you.

In writing this book, I want to do my part in saying thank you to the people who have inspired me and helped me directly and indirectly when it was most needed. I also want to inspire the future generation to fight through the tough times for a bigger and brighter future. Because the world needs more leaders and people doing the right thing now than ever before. Our generation is at a crucial moment to create an incredible impact on the future of many generations to come.

ABOUT THE AUTHOR

Sunil Kumar, CEO of Reliance Real Estate, is the recipient of numerous awards for his role in making Reliance the fastest-growing real estate company in Australia and New Zealand. Philosopher, inspirer, best-life enthusiast, Sunil is humbly dedicated to making all lives around him bigger and brighter.